IN MANY VOICES

—Our Fabulous Foreign-Language Press

By the author of

Brain-Washing in Red China

Brainwashing: The Story of
Men Who Defied It

The Story of Mary Liu

The Black Book on Red China

The Past Present:
A Year in Afghanistan

Biographical preface
for U Nu's play:
The People Win Through

IN
MANY
VOICES

—Our Fabulous Foreign-Language Press
By EDWARD HUNTER

Publisher:

NORMAN COLLEGE

Norman Park, Georgia

CONTENTS

Dedication

FOR DEDICATION, I INTENDED A FEW CRISP SENTENCES formally noting the role of Norman College, of Norman Park, Georgia, as sponsor of this little book. As my contact with Norman College grew, its fine spirit and lofty goals became more and more infectious. Now, as I write this, I want also to express my appreciation to its faculty and student body for the inspiration I received from their environment. I hope it is reflected in these pages.

Norman College is an expanding, Baptist-operated, accredited junior college of the new, modern type. Its American Culture Program, under which this project was undertaken, won first prize in a nationwide Freedoms Foundation contest.

These pages present a cross-section of the foreign-language newspapers in the United States. I am making no attempt at this time to include all of the forty or so languages in which these papers are published, and am also limiting this edition to the continental United States. I selected foreign-language groups with significant differences from among those communities where I had gathered the most information.

The only other book that attempted a comprehensive survey in this field was written almost forty years ago, in the turbulent post-World War I period, when Robert E. Park wrote his pioneering work, "The Immigrant Press and Its Control," published in 1922.

The press in those days meant newspapers. Now it embraces the whole realm of organized communication, including television and radio, newsmagazines and specialized bulletins. Each of these has become too big to be dealt with otherwise than separately.

If the material presented in these pages is sufficiently informative, thought-provoking, and perhaps controversial to arouse further inquiry, I shall feel well rewarded. I am thinking now of newspaper publishers and editors, as well as all those concerned with communications, the departments of journalism, history, sociology and political science in our educational institutions, political and business circles that are in contact with our minority groups, and of course, Americans generally who wish to be acquainted with this little known segment of our society.

I invite those who are connected with the foreign-language press to offer suggestions, corrections and data to improve these findings. Whatever help they can give in filling the gaps in this work, making it as accurate and balanced as possible, is earnestly sought.

Dr. Guy N. Atkinson, President of Norman College, deserves particular mention for his enthusiasm and encouragement. Dr. Eugene M. Keebler, Dean-Registrar, a young archaeologist, teacher of Greek and a practicing Minister of the Gospel on his week-ends, was most helpful in many practical matters. I am happy to have this opportunity to thank Col. James E. and Mrs. Evelyn Wilson for having brought me and

Norman College together. The cover design is by Mrs. Charles (Pauline) Hurst of Tifton, Ga.

I thank the staff of specialists and linguists at the Common Council for Nationalities Service in New York City for their cooperative spirit and for providing me with the statistics it compiled for as late as 1960.

All that appears under my name is my complete responsibility. As in all my writings, I have endeavored to utilize only firsthand sources, no matter how tempting the other material. Norman College, of course, is not responsible for any views expressed or errors I may have made.

EDWARD HUNTER

Moultrie, Ga.
May 15, 1960

Chapter One

Target: The Mind

1. THE AMERICAN MIRACLE

Americans are inclined to take the United States for granted, as they certainly do their own, hard-won liberties. Yet if we make believe that we are living some hundreds of years ago, and look out at the world as we would have viewed it then, with the restricted knowledge of those years, when ocean journeys took almost half a year, and everything else was in proportion, we will see as no less than a miracle our development as one nation, stretching from ocean to ocean, united in singleness of character, capable of producing a universally-recognized national type, the American citizen.

When we look at the map as it is now, and see the sweep of our continent-wide country, it might seem natural that we evolved as we did. But this backward glance shows very much that could not have even been suspected before. The United States in its present contours looks obvious to us now only because this is the way it happened. If it had developed differently, this is what would have appeared as natural, even inevitable. Yet how frequently, in those early centuries while we were a-borning, and during the years of our growing-up pains, would a slight impact, or lack of it, have drastically changed our whole course. History is packed with trivialities and casual choices that became turning points in our country's life. Indeed, it appears at times as if our great events are the outcome of little things, wholly dependent upon them, instead of it being the other way round. A word spoken or left unspoken, a minute—nay, a second—more or less, and our most important epochs would have developed differently. Benjamin Franklin flitted socially from drawing room to drawing room in London and Paris, which not done would have undone the American Revolution, for lack of the crucial French ally he gained thereby.

This vast stretch of territory which comprises the United States had every prospect of evolving as a conglomeration of small, bickering countries, each speaking its own language. Nothing would have seemed more natural, nothing would have been more readily understood today by the world and by ourselves than a division of the North American continent along numerous linguistic, nationalistic lines. This was the normal pattern of those crucial years, and history in this mid-Twentieth Century would be expressing no astonishment if it had evolved that way.

Indeed, if we think of the multitude of settlements that were established on New World soil by the various nations of Europe, and the many more that were so very nearly set up, and if we consider, too, the fiercely imperialistic, wholly self-centered drive of their motherlands, the miracle of it is obvious. We only narrowly escaped such a natural denouement, and this world would never have appreciated the utter tragedy of what could have been, but had been missed somewhere along the road, because someone was not quite as alert as he might have been, or someone's mood had been a little more or less dyspeptic, or a bullet had shifted a few inches more or less to one side.

This has been the thin reed upon which man's destiny has always leaned. Had Genghis Khan not succumbed to some plague when he did, all Europe likely would have become incorporated in Asia, as it was fast doing. If Alexander the Great had not fallen to some plague when he did, all the Middle East from Afghanistan to India would likely have evolved European. Destiny is a shake of the dice, as the Greek gods well knew, and man has the consolation of being given his turn in the game. Maybe this is our ultimate democracy, our shared stake with divinity.

Fortunately for man, he cannot know how many little things, handled a wee bit more purposefully, could have brought about some stupendous accomplishment. The agony of knowing one's missed opportunities would be too painful to bear. The same holds true for a nation.

Common sense and convenience seemed to make inevitable the occupation and development of our California coast by Spain centuries before any other people were anywhere ready. The most lush commerce of the world was then proceeding by galleon from Manila to Acapulco in Mexico, then New Spain. More accessible and better ports lay within sight to the northward. The traders had a couple of centuries in which to enter and make use of them. The royal court at Madrid had to be unbelievably inflexible, and the rivalry between grandees turned merchants had to be more petty than that of their most despised mestizos at the gaudy Acapulco fair grounds for this not to happen. Yet it didn't.

The Golden Gate lay invitingly in sight of galleon skippers sorely weary after five or more months on the eastward voyage, but they were under strictest orders to proceed. California was supposed to be one or more islands, of which the ocean was full. It were as if a knowing destiny was preserving this American soil for its own purpose. Otherwise, by the time our nascent United States had penetrated to the West, it would have been the oft-told Twentieth Century tale of too little and too late. All would have been Spanish —Spanish-speaking throughout and thoroughly Spanish in character.

San Francisco Bay was discovered by the Spaniards only in 1769, as a delayed reaction to Czarist Russia's creeping encroachment from the north.

If the Spaniards had obtained a whisper of the gold that was found barely a century later, the die would have been cast. As the Encyclopedia Britannica says, "If the Spanish settlers had discovered gold, the destiny of the province would have been different from what it proved to be; in that event it might have become a Spanish American Republic or England might have acquired it."

As it was, if Sir Francis Drake had not felt gorged with pirate loot, he would have gone beyond where he anchored in 1759, a few miles north of San Francisco harbor. Instead, he left a metal slab vaguely claiming all the region for Queen Elizabeth, which was not found until 1936 in Marin County. He preferred the prospect of capturing a fleeting galleon with its horde of treasure rather than lay an incontrovertible claim to the good earth of California.

Another stroke of incredible good fortune had to transpire in much the same area for our country to expand as it did. Russian settlements, reflecting the bravado and arrogance of a European imperial court but little removed from Asian despotism, were being established on Pacific coastal lands about the time the Thirteen States were experimenting with federal union. These Czarist settlements stretched around from the Arctic regions and spread down what is now the United States coastline.

They possessed for base a vast, impregnable fortress, now our new state of Alaska. The Russians set up a supply station and a vegetable farm for Alaskan traders and trappers at Ft. Ross, less than a hundred miles north of San Francisco.

Nothing, it seemed, could dislodge this colossus. Yet it took only a change in personnel in Russia to accomplish the abandonment of all these settlements in our Temperate Zone, opening the way for others to occupy the land.

As for Alaska, the inordinately proud Russian imperial family caught us unawares by offering to sell it all to us for a mere $7,200,000, when we had come only to ask for permission for some of our fur traders to go up there. The Czar by ukase in 1821 forbade navigators from approaching less than a hundred miles of his possessions.

The Czar, when he offered us this bargain, was thinking of his need for ready cash. Indeed, the major obstacle to the negotiations was not him. American pseudo-statesmen, who were too intent on today to spare a glance into tomorrow, made a demagogic effort to reap political hay out of the sale, ridiculing it as

"Seward's Icebox," branding it "Seward's Folly." The Senate very nearly rejected the whole deal. Fortunately we had for Secretary of State a man of policy and decision named William H. Seward, and there were no Hamlet postures in him; in spite of whatever other faults he had, he could say yes and make it stick, and he did so with the Alaska purchase.

The Russians left only a few orthodox churches as mementoes of their stay from Alaska to California. Otherwise Russian might have become the national language and the coloration of this great stretch of our West, of which Alaska alone was half the size of our Louisiana Purchase.

That vast heartland of our country, possibly the richest agricultural territory in the world, came to us by surprise, too. Indeed, our early history teaches that our greatest gains were achieved through our readiness to grasp opportunities as they arose. This required people with a capacity for leadership who accepted personal, individual responsibility as naturally as they did breathing. What a world apart from the faceless planning of the present-day committee system, with its watering down and discouragement of initiative!

Several centuries of enterprise appeared to have rewarded France with the entire broad stretch of richly fertile land down the center of the North American continent, with the Mississippi and the Missouri Rivers as its life-bestowing bloodstream. Indeed, Napoleon expected this possession to extend to the Rio Grande, through present-day Texas. The region was so enormous, much larger than the entire United States at the time, that there was every assurance of it becoming as French in language and outlook as Canada's Gaspé Peninsula.

Our Minister in Paris, Robert R. Livingston, asked Napoleon merely to sell us the mouth of the Mississippi River for a port. His usually astute Foreign Minister Talleyrand astonished our delegate by asking that we buy the entire territory—five times the size of continental France—for a mere $15,000,000—it proved to be 529,911,680 acres at four cents an acre. Even this sum was cut $3,750,000, to cover money owed by France to some of our citizens.

Livingston and James Monroe, who joined the negotiations, did not have instructions to discuss any such deal, nor the authority to do so. This technicality did not stop them. They signed anyway, without the slightest worry that the State Department, as undoubtedly would happen today, would rebuke them for exceeding their orders, and cancel the whole transaction. We luckily had not yet time to develop a bureaucracy. It was only 1803.

This great, good fortune can be traced to an insignificant defeat that some Negro troops under a colorful, black leader named Toussaint L'Ouverture dealt a batch of Napoleon's malaria-infested soldiers on Santo Domingo. Napoleon had been considering what is now the Dominican Republic and Haiti as the necessary base for this whole region, without which he lost interest in it.

If it had not been for this skirmish, the Corsican would never have abandoned his new, French world. Without it, the cramped United States would have lacked the prestige and strength to safely steer itself through the Napoleonic Wars between France and

England. With it, our dominance in North America was made certain.

New Orleans might have stayed Spanish, too, or it could have remained French. German-speaking and other European settlements on American territory would have followed the lead in becoming independencies or even principalities, and we can be sure, somewhere among all of these, England would have returned and secured a new foothold. How long the vulnerable, little United States on the northeastern coast could have stuck together or preserved its independence under such circumstances is anyone's guess. Surely it could not have been for long.

If there is, indeed, aspects of a miracle in the attainment of our national unity, our early Americans made themselves conscious vehicles of this great enterprise. They possessed the daring that is a pole apart from the conformism of the present, an intellectual courage that had great vision in it. They were precise thinkers, as demonstrated by a host of famous documents that came from their quills, which stand out to this day as unparalleled products of social and political thought.

The temperament and environment of the times allowed for no confused thinking. People with confused minds dropped by the wayside, dead. Before a man could be quick on the trigger, he had to think fast. The times required practical men even among theoreticians. They had to be individualists who knew what they wanted, and who could keep the national polity always in mind. They assumed personal responsibility as man's inherent right, and on this basis, were ready leaders. Those who pressed westward by foot, on horseback or by covered wagon well knew what they were after. As private individuals, each in his own right, they moved inexorably to their goal, creating the American type of character, fusing themselves into their vision.

They were strict in their standards, and all were welcome to take the same, hard road, each in his own stride and manner, if he possessed the capability. This was their tolerance and this their liberal outlook.

Out of this came the other part of the miracle, that so many diverse types of people from all parts of Europe—Englishmen and Hessians, Dutchmen and Poles— differing in the foods they ate, the clothes they wore, the languages they spoke, often differing in their interpretation of religion, did come together and merge their many differences in the political and social philosophy of George Washington, Thomas Jefferson, Ralph Waldo Emerson and David Henry Thoreau and the other clear-headed, liberal thinkers of the Republic's early life. They regarded clarity of mind as a manifestation of the divine. There was an august simplicity in their thinking. A fact was a fact for them, for they were legalists. Objectivity would never become a theoretical thing in their company, creating the confusion of double-talk and double-think. They demolished the Tower of Babel, for it was confusing, and the numerous languages thenceforth represented in our early immigration gave way, brick by brick, to English as the national tongue.

In this setting reposes the reason why our foreign-language press occupies such an exhilarating and generally speaking, constructive position in American society. Yet there probably is no segment of American

life about which less is known, or about which there
are more misconceptions. Particularly is its importance grossly underestimated. The foreign-language
press in America has always exerted immense influence either in the United States or abroad, and its
ramifications spread far, wide and deep.

The influence exerted on the "old country" by
foreign-language newspapers from America has in
some ways, too, been as great and even greater than
at home. They have been witting or unwitting vehicles
for the Americanization of their readers, while on the
other side of the ocean they started a ferment for the
modernization of language and ideas. A number of
European languages were given a stable form through
the creative release of the energies of immigrants in
America, expressed in their press. Into submerged
European nationalities the foreign-language papers
from America infused new life.

These characteristics developed normally and early
in the foreign-language press in America, becoming its
tradition. Like all genuine tradition, this arose spontaneously out of its environment. In a very real way,
these papers were missionaries of the American way
of life, giving rise to a restlessness and a vigor that
inevitably extended the freedoms enjoyed in the United
States. This is the heritage of our foreign-language
newspapers that makes it impossible for them to be
content with silence or a neutralist attitude toward the
plight of the captive peoples of the world. This is
part of their repayment to the United States for their
debt to America for giving a haven to the downtrodden
and to the oppressed of mind or body among their own
peoples.

The foreign-language newspapers learned how to mobilize public opinion and how to exercise political pressure. They went through a very practical experience to attain this status.

Initially they were torn between two poles, a sense of belonging and loyalty to the country where their editors and their readers were born, and a sense of belonging and loyalty, too, to the country which received them so openly. Most often they started out with only the former motive. Many, indeed, were the immigrants of both high and low station in life who came to America to make a fortune and then return to their native land, who remained in the United States and never went back. A combination of historic circumstances and the roots they gradually sunk into this new country, materially and spiritually, Americanized them. This happened to many who came to the United States intending only to use it as a base from which to continue the political struggle in their native land, who went through this same process and became American, whose descendents today are totally part of the American scene. There were others, of course, such as Bukharin and Trotsky, successively editor of the Russian-language Novy Mir (New World) in New York, who were utterly obsessed in their own schemings. When the moderate Kerensky revolution succeeded in St. Petersburg, they rushed there with nary a glance back, to help overthrow it in turn, giving power to the Bolsheviks.

Initially, the foreign-language papers represented the old ways and the old ideas, even the "old country," providing only such information about America as was absolutely necessary for their readers to know in order

to survive in this new country. But this little bit was
the decisive, opening wedge. The next stage was
reached when they realized that a man who was not
a United States citizen lacked influence and the benefits that came with it, and that one sure way to exert
influence in the American democracy was to get into
politics. Persons of their own background, they knew,
could best interpret and satisfy their yearnings. Who,
indeed, better than one of their own national origin?
Also, this would give them a share in the power. But
for this, one had to be a councilman, or a judge, or a
ward functionary. This meant not only taking out
"American papers" but blending into the American
scene.

Thus, partly consciously and partly through the
pressure of environment, the newspapers that survived
were in the main those that evolved this natural way,
that encouraged and helped their readers learn the
American way of life and become a part of it. Planning could never have evolved such a genuine article
as the resultant American citizen of, say Eastern European derivation. The Englishman went through
much the same process, often waiting many years before becoming a citizen of the United States.

2.   MORE THAN CLAY

The confrontation of numerous languages and nationality traits from all parts of Europe, with a Middle Eastern admixture and a smattering from Asia, as
well as the enforced African contribution, give particular poignancy to the legitimate question: "What is
an American?"

The pat reply is a legal definition. An American is anyone born on United States soil or who possesses American citizenship. But is this all that is necessary for a person to be truly American? Of course not; it is the technical and quantitative portion of it, leaving out the equally essential qualitative. There are responsibilities as well as rights involved, duties as well as privileges, an outlook as well as a physique. An American is immensely more than his "papers". What pinpoints a man as an American in the sight and opinion of his fellow American is his outlook and character, his bearing and conduct. Lack of it calls into question a man's qualifications as integrally an American. He can claim all the rights and privileges of citizenship, yes, indeed, but he is nonetheless an American only in part, in spirit a hyphenated American. Therein lies the hyphen.

American jurisprudence recognizes no hyphen; to be truly an American, one must owe his allegiance, under God, wholly to the United States, and to no other land or cause on earth. Americanism is sufficient cause, in conflict with none other that is good. There is harmony here with the demands of religion, for the American way of life specifically recognizes that a man's God is his own, personal concern, not a matter for governmental regulation or interference. Neither need violence be done to a person's forebears and their culture and country. He is to be pitied who lacks a sense of debt to his forebears. What America has done is to take unto its bosom, absorbing for its own good and prosperity, all that these other cultures can contribute. A Faust, Goethe, Pushkin,

Dante, Cervantes, yea, and a Confucius too, all can be translated with pride at the American table, along with Shakespeare, who belongs more directly to the American inheritance, and the teachings of our own Walt Whitman, Mark Twain, Edgar Allen Poe and Eugene O'Neil.

An American is more, too, than land, than even the soil of this country of our's. Under certain circumstances one need not be born on American soil to be an American. Our American land is the symbolic representation of American solidity and permanence. What is fundamental, too, is not one's racial tag or religious label. What is decisive is a man's attitude about these things, deep inside himself, how he reacts to the American environment and to his fellow Americans. This does not mean conformism, but being oneself, in a positive, honorable sense. All of this goes into the crucible, the melting pot, out of which is derived this complex human being, the true, integrated American.

The editor of one foreign-language newspaper told me: "At the end of my first week in the United States, I felt that this was the land where I should have been born." He recalled walking through the houses of Congress, aglow with the American spirit that allowed him to wander freely in its broad passageways. For the first time in his life, he felt he was in his own environment. The newspaper he edits, the Novoye Russkoye Slovo (The Russian Word), reflects this attitude of its editor, Mark E. Weinbaum, who makes a policy of explaining and interpreting what is peculiarly America, our electoral and other procedures, our customs and habits.

Novoye Russkoye Slovo does this in such an informative and encouraging manner that a patriotic American engineer of Russian extraction, a friend of mine, whose English is flawless, turns to it for objective details on such matters as election issues. The newspaper features special articles by informed observers and participants on facets of American life. Naturally, such a paper relentlessly fights the communist virus as it does anything it recognizes as anti-American.

Then there is the typical communist newspaper in America—any one of them. There isn't anything American in them except their address. They are representative of a sector of the foreign-language press in the United States about which the American public is generally ignorant and unconcerned, because these Communist organs are small and few. But there is a coordination to them, each in a different language and in a different industrial sector, that shows a tactical selection of publishing areas, those most highly dangerous to American security. Their staffs are permeated with "Fifth Amendment Americans", who take refuge in the American Constitution and in recent Supreme Court decisions, when their subversive and espionage activities for the Kremlin are referred to.

No, indeed, an American is neither a document, nor just soil, or anything wholly physical. An American is an idea, the embodiment of an idea. What makes an American are spiritual elements, mental reactors. These are so natural in him that they seem indistinguishable from physical reflexes, but they are sep-

arated by the infinite gulf that marks mind from
matter.

The freedom we enjoy came not from things but
from these spiritual concepts, the fruit of people's
thoughts, not of the soil; it is this that graphically
delineates the American as a personality. The United
States is testimony to the truism that people are
essentially the ideas we hold, and to which we give
expression in word and mortar, not just our physical
qualities. This, too, is what gives the foreign-language
newspapers in the United States their very special
responsibility.

What, then, is America, this land of ours? It, too,
is more than its soil, mountains and streams, grand
and inspiring though they be. Other lands, many with
vastly longer histories, situated on other fine conti-
nents, also are blessed with grandiose natural settings
and stupendous resources. Why have their people not
gained the same benefit from them that we have from
ours?

America, first and foremost, is people, the American people. The nation's personality is what makes
it distinctly American. Personality is its paramount
treasure, from which all else receives its measure.
This character comes solely from people. What the
soil, mountains and streams contribute is the setting
for this free environment, in which the untrammeled
energies of people are released. Our fantastic produc-
tion in material things and our unparalleled standard
of living are the consequence of the fulness and integrity of these released energies. Insofar as we lose
touch with them, be our wealth in industrialization
and mechanization ever so fabulous, we will go on

the downgrade, and material advantages will be powerless to slow the pace of it.

These released energies are our primary manufacture and our greatest resource. They derive from our motivations. What is called an inspiring scene, or an inspiring note, is blank and mute without such consummation which only man's released energies can give. He alone, by his attitudes and his reactions, transforms them into inspiration.

3. THE CONSTANT BARRAGE

More than ever, Americans are subjected to a constant barrage of appeals and pressures. They come from all directions, here and abroad. Every sphere of human thought and endeavor contributes to this unceasing onslaught against the mind of the ordinary man. Inexhaustible, ever-expanding channels of communication are made available by our modern press for a perpetual flow of publicity and propaganda. They are open to anyone who has anything to argue or to sell. Multi-million dollar professions exist solely by their know-how in the manipulation of attitudes. These techniques have spread in a steadily rising spiral from P. T. Barnum and his circus to Ivy Lee and his lush Wall Street accounts, leaped the gap into military service, and finally returned to civilian status in almost unrecognizable form, losing little time thereafter to jump into the political fray.

This has been a long development, going back many years. The great acceleration in its pace came only in its latter period, toward the close of World War I. From then on it kept gaining momentum.

Barnum, with his good-humored practices that exploited the simplicities in our early population, giving in return a fair measure of fun, has now turned into a grim technician who can't or won't distinguish levers and bolts from flesh and blood. His obsession in the techniques of his profession makes him particularly vulnerable to manipulation by outside influences. The communists have been anxious to exploit this opportunity. The English-language press is the main outlet in America for all these drives, good and bad. A constant competition between them is going on all the time. The confusion created by this steady barrage of conflicting claims has a benumbing effect, yet has become inescapable. No wonder mental health has become a new issue and a national concern.

The foreign-language press is not immune to these influences. Advantage has been taken of its comparative isolation, to use it as a channel for some of the more virulent conspirational drives. In addition to normal pressures, the foreign-language press is subjected to those peculiar to their own nationality groups, which often are the more intense.

All these forces from all directions constantly assault the mind of the foreign-language reader. Routine American influences, and they are myriad, seek to capture his attention. This is the American way. The conflict between different thought patterns adds to the turmoil. In the case of the many tens of thousands who have escaped from totalitarian countries, who never knew what it is to be given a choice, much less be besieged by many sides to pick and choose in every sphere, it is a frightening experience. Tragically panicked by it, some have fled back to the hell they hate but know.

Each man is on his own here, the butt of innumerable pressures related to his own environment, some natural and praiseworthy, while others seek to break or subvert his will. The motives behind the various appeals and pressures may themselves be confused, reflecting uncertainty at the source. Or they may be disguised. They can be broadly generalized under two headings, the pro-American and the non-American influences.

Each of these fall into various subdivisions. One sector of the foreign-language press seeks more or less successfully to be indistinguishable from an ordinary English-language paper in everything except language. Another section is intensely nationalistic as regards country of origin, while vehemently in support of American policies. Efforts are more or less subtly made by still another faction to maintain foreign nationalist ties and loyalties, becoming representative not of the American press in a foreign language, but constituting a foreign press on American soil.

Outright examples of these are now exceedingly few, although there were many in the past. Either they faded out because they were not in touch with realities even in their own language community, or they grew out of this immaturity. In some papers, remnants of dead causes or past systems linger on, expressing perhaps Fascist-like sentiments in shrill, hateful terminology, or maybe lethargically recalling the luster of the Russian Czar. Finally, of course, there is the pink sector of the press, infiltrated by communism, as well as the small Red press whose

importance is derived from its conspirational connections and extra-curricular activities, not from normal considerations such as circulation and advertising.

The foreign-language paper is frequently identified more closely and more belligerently with nationality pressure groups than the English-language
press is with the political party of its preference—if
any. When not openly identified this way, they can
be spottily so, trapped into it by such vulnerabilities
as financial stringency, for the foreign-language newspaper is chronically "broke".

The reader of a foreign-language newspaper is
like a small boy in a five-and-ten-cent store, clasping
a dime in his hand. The toys and candies are dis-
played in tempting profusion and they all attract him,
appealing to his undeveloped mind. He wants to see
them all, walks back and forth, stares and touches.
All of them may be said to be competing to be bought;
each seeks to capture his mind. They have many
forceful lures: pretty packaging, the promise of fla-
vor and excitement, satisfaction for his childhood de-
sires. Yet he has only one thin dime clenched in his
little fist. What will he select? Will he actually suc-
ceed in making his own selection, or be awed by all
this gorgeous display, and end up by picking what
isn't good for him, or something that he never would
have chosen in a calmer moment

So it is with the competition between the numerous
pressures that compete for the mind of the reader
of our foreign-language press. Only this competition is
immensely more fierce. While most of it is openly
expressed and aboveboard, like the toys and candies
in the display counters, some of it is clandestine,

questionable goods concealed "under the counter." Some seek to take advantage of his "greenness" to put across frauds or unsavory and un-American objectives. Practically all the appeals and pressures try to use the thought patterns familiar to him. They deliberately evoke his nostalgia for old-time surroundings. His choice may very well determine his future. His welfare, and to this degree the welfare of the country where he has settled, and of which, purposely or willy-nilly he is now a part, are involved in it. He cannot avoid choosing, for failure to do so, or even delaying it, has its own consequences, the same as a choice.

Stranded in the midst of all these strange pressures, he tries to figure out the motive of each. There are so many conflicting counter-claims and counter-charges. Crucial and distracting elements come and go. The objectives behind the various pressures are not easily discerned. Maybe they can be plainly described, and are perfectly proper, but how can he tell? He is suspicious of them all. Wherever possible he finds some society or association where he can meet people of his own background, and receive their guidance. This has been the usual course.

Robert E. Park points out in his "The Immigrant Press and Its Control," published back in 1922: "Every language group in the United States maintains some sort of nationalist organization. These societies either establish journals of their own or they make some journal already established theirs."

This highly complex situation puts a particular burden on the foreign-language editor. His paper becomes a focal point for all such influences.

The foreign-language subscriber expects much more from his paper than the reader of an English-language paper. His dependence is greater, and his interest frequently wider. When immigration was at its height, and the reader of a foreign-language paper was a recent arrival, his demands were simple. He sought guidance in matters of livelihood, and help in his adjustment problems. He looked for direction in his relationship with authorities on the local and national level. He wanted his rights and privileges explained to him, and also wanted to know what was expected of him. The minority-language paper acted as a liaison for him, as his intermediary. His attitude toward the United States was influenced to a greater or lesser extent by what he learned from it.

The fundamental health and strength of the American way of life is demonstrated by how overwhelmingly, and how comparatively soon, despite all these complex and confusing pulls, the great proportion of our new arrivals became part of the American social and political environment. They became as American as their neighbors, reading the English-language press, keeping up-to-date on sports and zestfully following American politics, often participating, becoming judges, mayors and senators, even Presidential cabinet members. Many of these, as any other American might take advantage of the opportunity to expand his horizon, continue as subscribers to the foreign-language paper they saw in their home as youngsters, or that keeps them in touch with happenings abroad which have an influence on what takes place right here in the United States.

Chapter Two

Voice of the Minorities

1. MORE THAN SEMANTICS

One of the biggest surprises people get when the foreign-language press in America is discussed is to learn how big it is. Most persons think there are only a few such papers and that almost all are published in New York City. Actually, 65 newspapers were being printed daily in 1960 in 20 languages other than English in 21 cities. Of these, New York City produced 19 in 11 languages.

Chicago followed closely with nine dailies in six tongues. San Franciso had eight in four, Cleveland four in four, Boston four in three, Philadelphia three in three, and Los Angeles three in two languages. Fourteen cities have one foreign-language daily each, ranging from Portuguese in New Bedford, Mass., and Slovak in New York City to Japanese in Seattle and French in Fall River, Mass.

Chinese led with 10 dailies when 1960 began, but lost two in February, tying Spanish with eight. Polish followed closely with seven, Japanese six, Russian five, Italian and Jewish four each, German and Lithuanian three each, Armenian, Czech, Greek, Hungarian, Slovene and Ukrainian two each, and one each for Arabic, Finnish, French, Portuguese and Slovak.

Six dailies disappeared during the past year, or changed over to less frequent publications. Besides the two Chinese, these were one Spanish, one Serbian and two Finnish. The attrition in this field is unrelenting.

Foreign-language communities are particularly strong in weeklies, a number appearing twice or three times a week. The American Council for Nationalities Service, in New York City, lists 217 weeklies in 33 languages, including the Gazette Van Detroit (Detroit Gazette), the only Flemish periodical in America, that began in 1914, and has 5,000 circulation.

The Welsh have a language-publication, too, Y Drych, that goes back to 1851, a monthly published in Utica, N. Y., with 2,750 circulation.

The weeklies include 33 in German, 22 in Italian, 21 each in Polish and Spanish, and 20 in Hungarian. While Swedish has no daily, it has 10 weeklies. Two of the German weeklies actually are Swiss, and in addition the Germans have one semi-weekly and one tri-weekly. Twenty-eight other papers appear in 14 foreign languages, mostly as semi-weeklies, the others as tri-weeklies.

Typically the Swedish American community produces six weeklies in English. Only the Germans have more English-language weeklies, seven. All are religious, although one stresses news with a crusader's fervor. Altogether, 31 weeklies are published in English by 14 foreign-language minority groups.

Thirty-seven of the foreign-language weeklies appear in 13 tongues that have no dailies. A total of 655 foreign-language periodicals are listed in 38 languages, and 134 more are put out in English by nationality groups on the American mainland. The latter includes 13 semi-monthlies, 53 monthlies, 12 bi-monthlies, 15 quarterlies and 10 others.

A big proportion of the non-dailies, including a strikingly large number of the weeklies, are sponsored by religious associations, while another large fraction, that includes many dailies, are linked to fraternal or other nationality societies, an important segment of which are politically motivated.

What is obvious is that wherever any sizeable number of persons speaking a foreign language congregated, practically their first reaction to the American environment was to publish a newspaper. The nationality groups, from whichever part of the world they came, possessed a homogenity that needed only the free air of the New World to develop self-expression. A whole community of immigrants would often come from some one region, and in this new American atmosphere show an initiative that it had never known it had.

Newspapers were published by language groups that never had a paper, as with some of the Slavic peoples, who had not been allowed publications in their own tongue. In some instances, as in Jewish, an editor had to create his language as he went along, infusing into it the modernisms and the flexibility in which new ideas and technological terms could be presented, at the same time helping build up a literature for it.

These newspapers had a terrific impact when they were mailed back to the towns and villages in Europe from which these people had emigrated. The ferment, once started, went on its course impossible to undo or impede, spreading throughout the Old World's social and political structure.

The immigrants were anxious to see conditions improved in the "old country". Practical issues, about which they had strong feelings, cried out for discussion and settlement. Many of these people, perhaps most of them, expected to return there some day, although comparatively few did.

While the American public knew all about its missionaries in Asia and Africa, it had no idea of the simultaneous missionizing it was doing in backward Europe through the intermediary of these immigrants and their foreign-language papers. Whether the impact of these papers wasn't as great as that of the missionaries may be argued, but the record shows that the foreign-language press unmistakably left enduring marks socially and politically.

Twelve Slavic languages account for nearly one third of the total number of publications, from the old-fashioned, largest-sized dailies to monthly and quarterly magazines. About 20 of the languages are of peoples under Soviet domination, and represent fully 40 per cent of all the periodicals. The greater part of these are anti-communist, and represent the most knowledgeable and alert element in the United States as regards communist politics and Red tactics generally.

Those who come from lands dominated by the communists are also the most vocal in spotting and exposing Red maneuvers. While on the one side they display a wholesome, American outlook in their writings, on the other side they see clearly through the situation in the land of their forebears because of their lifelong, intimate relationship with its people, sometimes still continued through every variety of underground and circuitous channel. They are frankly stirred by the basic issue of the day—the preservation of American freedoms and the restoration of freedoms abroad where they have been crushed. This is no academic subject with these people; it is of their own flesh and blood.

There are few if any major modifications in communist strategy that have not been detected beforehand by these foreign-language papers, and ample warning given, if only they had been heeded. They recognize the tactics, from having seen them craftily employed in their own countries of origin, not only by the Reds but also by the Nazis and Fascists. Often, having lost their liberty after having had a taste of it, they are more vigilant about it than many Americans who can trace their ancestry back to our early history, but lack the firsthand experience of these newcomers. If these foreign-language publications can be said to have one paramount message, it is that nothing is more dangerous than to take freedom for granted. They have seen the Red juggernaut.

Hardly any group of persons could be found in America who have proved themselves to be the equals of these editors in appraising communist policy and activity, yet though practically every city and town has forums at which theroeticians from college campuses and social clubs gather to discuss the Soviet bloc, rarely is a foreign-language editor invited. Because of their personal involvement, their forewarnings have been ignored as biased, and their presence at forums excluded as "controversial." Invaluable material fails to reach the general public where it might do the most good.

The much smaller, pro-communist element in the foreign-language press measures its impact in other ways. Through its interlocking relationship with the communist movement generally, it can exert an influence of which the immensely more representative foreign-language groups are deprived. The latter operate each by itself, in the American manner, with only slight if any connection with each other, for the most part isolated from the English-language press as well, and unknown to the average American.

The American environment has had an ambivalent effect. While providing a channel for Americanization, it has also been a vehicle for intensified nationalistic feelings in these various foreign-language communities. While in the process of adapting himself to the American way of life, the newcomer was likely at the same time to want to see the same blessings of social and political liberties conferred upon his native land. There need be no conflict in loyalties. The United States has been both importing and exporting ideas ever since colonial days; indeed, if it hadn't been for the import of republican thought from such countries as France, although an emperor still reigned in Paris, and democratic views from England, it would have been impossible for the fathers of the American state to accomplish the rounded job they did. This give and take is still going on.

If it had not been for this continuing American interest and influence in foreign affairs, Czechoslovakia and Israel, to name the two most obvious, would probably not have become internationally recognized countries. The foreign-language press has had a crystallizing effect in all these movements. The Czech press has a longtime record of pro-democratic agitation, and its impact was a decisive element at the Versailles Peace Conference, where the just-born Czechoslovakia was baptized.

The Polish-language press at about the same time played a most important role in the rebirth of the martyred Polish nation in 1919. The American Poles sent their magnificent pianist, Ignace Paderewski, to Warsaw to be premier and foreign minister. The Italian-language press played a decisive role soon after World War II by instigating a letter-writing campaign by Americans of Italian ancestry in the United States, that succeeded in alerting the people of Italy, foiling a communist conspiracy to seize the country through the disarming medium of the ballot box.

The word "press" originally meant just newspapers—they are printed on a press. The word has since smashed out of this shell to become part of a vast, new world. The tremendous technical improvements made in communications during the past generation or two have extended the scope of the press to all organized or periodical media utilizing the written or spoken word. Newspapers, trade publications, specialized or behind-the-scenes bulletins that are only the size of a mimeographed sheet, radio and television and documentary films, all these have been swept

within the folds of the press. All became the tools
of the circus barker who turned publicity man, public
relations officer and then consultant, and in a quick
switch, a propaganda expert and psychological warfare specialist. The commercial uses of publicity were
developed in the United States, but they were bor-
rowed everywhere for absorption into military science.
We never caught up with this phase of it. Our democratic society has a built-in antagonism against
such trifling in human relations. But we were forced
to try timidly to keep pace with it, if only for self-
preservation's sake.

The "living newspaper" that briefly flourished in
the first Roosevelt administration in the mid-30s was
a dramatic form developed by experimentalists in the
theater in Germany. They were led by Communist
Party members and sympathizers, who used topical
subjects and kept dialogue up-to-date in the manner
of a newspaper meeting deadlines. This, too, was part
of the new press, at the same time incorporating it
into psychological warfare.

The phenomenal expansion in the reach of the press
began soon after the Versailles Peace Conference,
and went on at a steadily rising crescendo until World
War II removed all brakes. The press was given
literally unlimited scope and made the most of it.
Public relations walked arm in arm with propaganda warfare, that developed into psychological warfare, fully-grown twins of gargantuan proportions.
They became so swollen as to be almost uncontrollable.
Since the end of World War II they have had a tendency to fly off at tangents, dragging their masters
behind them.

Every possible means of getting a message across to a chosen audience, referred to behind a screen of professional unconcern as "the target", is nowadays indiscriminately seized upon and exploited. Friend or foe is beyond the point. The technique has become the thing, supposed to relieve one of responsibility, as unmoral as a robot. The target—customer or subject—has to be convinced, or overcome, and this is all that matters. This steers its technicians into a mad logic that puts a patriot and a traitor on a par. Both brush their teeth, so a toothpaste advertising campaign must be careful not to offend either. Autos become, through the magic of this compound of circus barker and propaganda pressure specialist, no longer a convenience to get as quickly and smoothly as possible from one place to another, but a phallic symbol.

The end of the war saw a shift of personnel out of the psychological warfare sections of Free World governments and into commercial life, taking these wartime tactics with them. The communist bloc continued its wartime bureaus as heretofore, merely changing the name of the play from "War" to "Peace."

Little imagination was needed to visualize the dangerous shoals that lay ahead, at home and abroad, and they weren't long in appearing. Domestically, they took such ghastly shapes as subliminal perception, and adopted such sanctimonious poses as social engineering. All of these pressure mechanisms looked upon the press as a made-to-order manipulation channel. On the world scene, they enabled the Kremlin to move from one war-like victory to the other.

Our foreign-language radio and television could rightly be included in any such survey as this. Many stations and programs operate in conjunction with newspapers. They have grown so enormously, however, that they just have to be dealt with separately.

A total of 624 radio stations were broadcasting foreign-language programs in the United States last year in 45 languages, from Basque and Gaelic to Slovene and Turkish. They emanated from hundreds of localities. Spanish led here, too, with an astounding 283 stations carrying its programs, closely followed by the Italian with 149. Hindustani had a station at Yuba City, Cal., and Maltese in Detroit. Most of these stations broadcast programs in a number of languages.

The American Indians can listen to 16 stations broadcasting in their own languages, such as Navajo, Ute, Zuni, Apache and Hopi. These can hardly be included among foreign-language programs. The American Indians could justifiably say it was the other way round; that their's are the only native languages heard over the air in America!

These statistics cannot give any accurate idea of the proportion of listeners, which depends on number of hours of programming and density of population. Russian is heard, for instance, only over six stations, the Jewish language over 31, but most of these are in the main population centers, where a great mass audience is ready at hand.

2. PROBLEMS OF SURVIVAL

The foreign-language newspapers were started by immigrants for immigrants, and remained so until about World War I. Up to then, as soon as one reader acquired enough American habits and learned enough English to subscribe to an English-language paper, another immigrant or perhaps two came along to replace him. But not any more. Immigration has slowed down to a trickle since this peak, when the packed holds of ocean liners steamed with their presence, and Ellis Island was a beehive of aliens being processed and documents being stamped.

The ordinary immigrant of those days came to the United States with the open, inquisitive mind of the peasant or village worker, unencumbered by more than the simple folklore and the strict code of conduct he had picked up at his childhood heath. The adjustment problem was much more complicated for the later intellectual. He belonged to the scholarly classes, or his family had held a government post. His mind, while not closed, was partially filled with vested loyalties that clashed with his new approach. He had a great deal to unlearn. The changeover had to be a deliberate exertion of will in his case, not always without anguish, in contrast with the natural acceptance of the New World by his simpler minded countryman.

This raises a question that only the future will answer, concerning the relative adjustability into American life of the untutored, uncultured immigrant we used to have, who came with only ready hands and an eager mind, or the highly skilled, often sophisticated immigrant our technological screening process brings in these days. There is much to be said on both counts.

Immigration remains an important factor in some nationality groups, but isn't any longer the exclusive factor. In an increasing number of nationality groups it isn't even the paramount factor. Most of the present-day immigrants from Germany and Italy, for example, step off the gangplank of their plane or ship speaking at least some English. They walk up to a newsstand and buy an English-language paper. In contrast with the old immigration, the intellectuals who constitute today's arrivals come with established standards and cultural demands. They complain that the German writing is stilted, or that the Italian is boorish, because it sometimes isn't exactly the same as in Berlin or Rome. There is good reason for the difference. These papers are written for a local clientele, and the writing has been adapted to the needs and speech of the established community.

In overall figures, foreign-language newspapers have declined markedly in numbers over the past half century. Government agencies and the Common Council compiled a list in 1942 showing a total of 96 dailies and 498 weeklies and semi-weeklies. In 1960 there were about 30 less dailies and a decrease of nearly a half in weeklies and semi-weeklies. The significance of this can be easily exaggerated, for the circulation of foreign-language papers of all descriptions in 1942 was estimated at 6,704,360, while Common Council figures put it still at 6,084,026 last year. Compared with the 1920s, however, there undoubtedly had been a more pronounced drop.

N. W. Ayer's directory gave the figure for January, 1920, as 7,618,497, not too striking a difference with the latest statistics, considering the more careful watch kept nowadays to prevent brazen falsification. Park, in his book said that total circulation for that year was estimated as high as 10,000,000, but warned of gross exaggeration.

Overall figures, large or small, are little comfort to the editor of a minority-language newspaper who knows that his own circulation has taken a dive. The difference is made up by new readers added in other nationality groups. The recent Puerto Rican influx, for instance, has provided the 60,000 circulation attained by El Diario de Nueva York (New York Spanish Daily). The flow of refugees and displaced persons into the United States in the past couple of decades has been a boon to the Slavic press, while the Hungarian papers gained a little from the immigration that followed the Free World's abandonment of the victorious Freedom Fighters to Soviet Russian tanks.

Nowhere is there such a fluctuation in circulation as in the foreign-language field. In order to meet the demands of his readership, the foreign-language editor has to make himself indispensable to his community in the manner of the traditional, American smalltown editor. Individuality, increasingly disappearing from the syndicate-ridden English-language press nowadays, is still the hallmark of the foreign-language paper. Indeed, almost only in the foreign-language newspaper offices can one find the atmosphere of the old Park Row, when it was the home of New York's largest dailies.

The second-generation reader is the perennial headache of the foreign-language editor. Yet somehow, those papers that courageously present the American scene, instead of seeing their subscribers flock to the English-language press, are the ones that best withstand the ebb flow in immigration, who hold longest to their readers, and are best able to survive.

Yet every editor watched a goodly number even of the first generation leave him. As the years went by and the alien slowly picked up English, he was inclined to turn to the simpler-worded and the more sensational of the English-language papers. They were being skillfully tailored to his wants and yearnings. They helped him learn English, too. Once the immigrant acquired sufficient English, if he continued reading his foreign-language paper, it was because it carried news of fraternal groups and covered international affairs in greater depth. Nothing the foreign-language editor did could halt the trend. All his ingenuity was not enough to hold the eager newcomer.

He saw the second generation swallowed up in the English-speaking environment, contributing to the new American type into which it was merging. The melting pot was no mere figment of speech to the editor on the scene. The young man or young lady born here of alien parents was determined not to be a "foreigner." He or she turned to English completely.

Into this situation, more and more foreign governments have delved through their information programs that include news bulletins and other periodicals sounding the nostalgic appeal of the "old country." Up to a point, of course, this is acceptable and even desirable, for our friendly relations with other countries can have no stronger bond than this people-to-people affinity of mutually admired historical and cultural links. If it begins to impinge on matters of loyalty and security, it is something else again. The communist bloc, for instance, has been engaged for years in a highly organized redefection campaign, with a headquarters in East Germany that publishes newspapers purporting to come from each of the satellite countries. These are sent into the United States by the bale. The locally-printed communist press works in close relationship with this openly subversive press. While the latter openly urges the refugee to come back, the former supports this appeal with glowing pictures of prosperity and happiness being enjoyed by all in the "old country," while selecting only those items about America that present us in the worst possible light.

This problem reflects the rise, too, of nationalist feelings in practically all these groups, and the great skill being applied nowadays in re-awakening and intensifying these attitudes. This sort of propaganda and covert pressure is nothing new. Foreign governments have been caught a number of times trying to exert influence on its emigrants in America through our foreign-language press. This was often crudely attempted, as by the Kaiser and Hitler in World Wars I and II, and by the Austro-Hungarian Empire even before World War I. Arab and Middle Eastern governments, exploiting the advantage that the tight Moslem religion provides them as a control channel, have frequently utilized the foreign-language press in America. Zionism is a bridge for Israel. Where church and state are interwoven, it is impossible to draw the line where the influence of one ends and the other begins. This is a matter of conscience that defies any pat solution by formula. The only standard for judgment becomes a moral and a practical one at the same time, depending on goodwill and adaptability to the American way of life. There are many issues in life before which man's finite mind can best make an ally of time, and these problems are among them.

Editors first sought to solve their dilemma by giving over part of their space to articles and editorials written in English. Advertisements often included English phrases. This sometimes was the first English to appear in a foreign-language paper. These advertisements were among the most popular part of a paper, for they were used as English-language lesson sheets.

Sometimes the editor gave over a full page or half the paper to English. Logically, this should have solved his problem, but reality has an impish way of man-handling logic. Mixed daily papers, except in some specialized situations, satisfied neither the one nor the other, and the expedient has been often abandoned. They frequently flourish as weeklies, though. One publishing house in Calumet, Mich., decided it had to be one or the other and started publishing separate papers on April 16, 1959. The Copper County News was begun as an Anglo-Finnish weekly in English, with emphasis on Finnish fraternal and other news, in twelve big, old-fashioned, folio pages, set by hand. The Finnish weekly from which it stemmed changed its name to American Sanomat (Finnish American News), adding "American" to its title. Each claims about 3,000 circulation.

A novel expedient was tried by a Serbian newspaper with an English, mid-week supplement that published daily except Saturday and Sunday. Leaving the daily field, it changed to a semi-weekly, making its

English supplement a separate, weekly paper. This is Amerikanski Srbobran (American Srbobran), that began in 1906, and is the organ of the Serb National Federation, with 12,000 circulation for both Serbian and English editions.

The expertly edited New Yorker Staats-Zeitung und Herold (New York State Journal and Herold) experimented with an English-language section, providing it with a fine staff. Yet to no avail; it was a waste of pages to those who could read only German, and a waste, too, to those who knew English, for they preferred a whole paper to half a one. The fact was that once a subscriber was able to read English, the nationality paper simply couldn't compete in providing the all-around news and features that helped him feel at home in America. The English-language newspaper was the symbol that a person had to read in order to cross the divide.

As circulation fell, foreign-language dailies shortened into weeklies, semi-weeklies and tri-weeklies. Sometimes they left the news field entirely, changing into a religious, cultural or fraternal periodical, with a magazine format, frequently patterned after the newsmagazines. This way the foreign-language papers could hope to retain those readers whose outlook had widened and who could no longer be expected to depend on them, with their restricted coverage, for the general run of the news.

Editors discovered that while the rank and file vanished into the seemingly bottomless pit of the American melting pot, the appeal of ancestral traditions did carry weight, particularly among the intellectual element in the second, and sometimes even in the first and third generations, too. They were urged to remain proud of their old customs and traditions, and not to be ashamed of their group characteristics and old loyalties. Those who wished, for sentimental or political reasons, to keep these memories alive, helped sponsor such publications.

A number of them are religiously orientated. The primary role that the church played in our colonial history survives in this form in the newer American communities. In some religious groups there is rivalry between those who focus on the New World and those who consider Europe first.

Foreign-language papers that turned into fraternal or even scholarly journals, in their own tongue, bilingually or in English, were able to do so usually because of a connection with some nationality society. This was a natural relationship where a community revolved around a church or welfare organization, the latter itself often associated with a religious body.

Membership in the society often included the subscription price of the newspaper or other periodical. Without this guaranteed circulation, many journals would have gone out of existence. Sometimes a newspaper regularly gave over an entire page, or two adjoining pages, to a nationality association for its announcements and news items, in return for being recognized as its official organ, with a guaranteed subscription. This is done, too, by communities that seek to maintain unity in face of some grave issue facing their ancestral land, when a crusading interest is being taken in it even by those who retain only a limited knowledge of the language.

An important number of nationality groups are now large and old enough to be publishing almost every type of paper and periodical in both the original tongue and English. Some magazines they put out are of the highest caliber, comparing favorably with similar-type publications coming off the American university presses. The Ukrainian Quarterly is one of these. This community has been revitalized by an inflow of inflexible anti-communists. Under robust and intelligent leadership, it has reversed the downward trend, raising the circulation of its various publications. Its 40 periodicals in 1959 had a total circulation of above 100,000, compared to only 14 periodicals with a 60,000 circulation in 1942. Its two dailies are Svoboda (Liberty), of Jersey City, N. J., begun in 1893, claiming 20,000 circulation, and Ameryka (America), of Philadelphia, begun in 1913, having 10,000 distribution. The latter gives some of its space over to English.

A number of foreign-language papers have settled upon a first-page column in English patterned after the late Arthur Brisbane's, or they print an editorial or two in English. Often this indicates a hard-hitting paper with a dignified format. Its editorial writer may produce exhaustive material not found in the English-language press, doing so forcibly and thoughtfully. Such a man is usually a leader in the community.

Another reason for the editor's viewpoint being presented in English is for the influence it can exert at City Hall, in the State Capital or at Washington. Many legislators and others in public life keep careful contact with the foreign-language press. An editorial in English makes the liaison easier, and is frequently quoted as representative of the thinking of the group. When the editor is unquestionably a highly respected leader, as is Ignace Morawski of Nowy Swiat (Morning World), a Polish daily of 24,000 circulation in New York City, his column in English is read very seriously in informed sources. Officials have learned that their election or appointment can be greatly or decisively influenced by the attitude of the nationality group. Editorials, while declining in influence in the increasingly impersonal English-language press retain their old-time effect in foreign-language papers. Their readers when displeased are likely not to wait to write a letter, but come striding to the editor's desk, confident of receiving a respectful hearing.

An example of the newer generation's exhilarating approach is provided by the English-language Arab weekly, the Lebanese American Journal, along with its parent paper, Al-Hoda (Guidance), the only Arabic daily in the United States. The same family has published them both since the latter was founded nearly sixty years ago in Philadelphia by Nahoum A. Mokarzel, who became an enterprising journalist, although a first-generation American. Both papers have always had an outspoken Christian orientation. On the founder's death, his brother, Salloum, succeeded him, to be followed in turn by his daughter, Mary, who became publisher of both and the editor of the English-language weekly, each of which has a 3,000 circulation. Another Arabic weekly, The Caravan, also in English, is published in Brooklyn, and claims 4,000 circulation.

The Lebanese American Journal courageously revealed that the dispatch of American Marines to Lebanon and then their quick withdrawal left the Lebanese

Christians, who had demonstrated their pro-Western sentiments and friendship for America, dangerously out on a limb. "We are in trouble because the Christians sided with America," one letter it published frankly said. Later, at the time of the bloody Iraq coup d'etat, the newspaper showed its spirit, too, by appealing for aid to Iraq's American-educated Foreign Minister, Fadhel Jamali, who had been a consistent Free World supporter. Now that he was in a desperate plight because of this friendship, he was being ignored to languish in prison and be sentenced to death—the sentence was commuted in 1960. "Where is the United States now? Where is Lebanon now? Why don't they lift a finger to help?" the little paper cried out while Fadhel Jamali was awaiting trial.

These editorials were typical instances of minority press efforts against overwhelming odds to influence events at home and abroad, on the basis of the fuller information which its intimate contacts give it, and its better knowledge of the psychological warfare effect of our action or inaction. The effectiveness of these efforts is linked to the size of the voting community involved, the accuracy of their views often being regarded as almost irrelevant.

In its own backyard, the Lebanon American Journal has been consistently preaching the American way of life. A typical editorial, picked almost at random, was entitled: "Good Citizenship." It told its readers that "the exercise of the franchise is the cornerstone of our democracy," adding: "Interest in government is one of the safeguards of our country as well as a demonstration of good citizenship. And not to vote is to indicate an attitude not appropriate to the democracy in which we are lucky enough to live."

In the tradition of American journalism, the little tabloid ran this challenge: "If you crave propaganda . . . if you desire slanted news . . . if you want to be misinformed . . . don't read the Lebanon American Journal."

The Arabic press has eight weeklies. Two out of four in New York are in English. One out of two in Detroit is bilingual. Detroit also has a semi-weekly, and nearby Highland Park, two weeklies, including Al Mashriq (The Orient), that claims 5,000 circulation. New York has the tri-weekly Meraat-Ul-Gharb (Mirror of the West), that began back in 1899. All these are in Arabic.

The problem of language is a heart-breaker for editors whose deep attachment to their mother tongue has been kept in full bloom by their use of it in journalism. They may know themselves to be loyal Americans, yet are pained by the thought of giving up this precious vehicle. I have heard the position taken that any language spoken by an appreciable sector of the American people is entitled to be recognized as one of the national languages of the United States. Yet it was not difficult to see that here was another instance of logic being pursued to an illogical extreme.

Language is an essential unifying factor in the United States, which more than any other land on earth is subject to extraordinary stresses and strains projected by its heroic welcome to all peoples alike to share in its blessings. The additional pressure that abandonment of such a fundamental unifying channel as a single, national language would entail would be suicidal.

In America, language may be compared to the mortar between our half a hundred states, holding the bricks together that compose our country's spiritual structure.

The complications that arise in our unprecedented unifying process, and the challenge to it, is vividly demonstrated by the situation in one of the most spirited segments of our foreign-language press, the newspapers printed in Spanish.

Chapter Three

The Spanish Imprint

The term Spanish-language press is only the start at its identification. There is a Puerto Rican press, a Cuban press, a Latin American press and a Mexican press, but no Spanish press, strictly speaking. These show colloquial differences, in the same way that American English isn't the same as British English.

More daily newspapers are published in Spanish than in any other foreign language in the United States, forging ahead only lately, replacing the German which for generations had the most papers and was the most widely circulated. The Spanish have eight dailies to the German three, but are behind in weeklies, 21 in that language to 33.

The tiny island of Puerto Rico, which we won from Spain in 1898, is responsible for this sudden rise. Nearly 700,000 Puerto Ricans now live in New York City, where there were hardly any a generation ago, and 200,000 others have moved on to other localities. The greatest number is crowded into one section of Manhattan island, alongside Harlem, although they have now taken over a number of other districts as well, and have spread into practically every area in the city where a building could be sub-divided into one-room flats.

The airplane made this precipitous influx possible by providing a steady flow of quick and easy flights. Rent control made New York City practical,

and keeps it so. A petty demagogue named Vito
Marcantonio saw a source of quickly attainable political power in this precipitous inflow of Puerto Rican
voters.

The recruitment of cheap agricultural labor for
the Middle Eastern states, aided by drummers for
airline business, gave the migration its original impetus. This was the modern version of the previous
century's recruitment of labor in East Europe and
Asia.

Like these predecessors, the Puerto Ricans wrote
home to their densely over-populated villages of primitive huts about the fabulous incomes available in this
new world, laying the groundwork for the really big
movement.

The Puerto Ricans were migrants, not immigrants,
although hardly any other people have ever willingly
entered the American mainland with as little knowledge of modern manners. They were granted American citizenship in 1917. Thereafter they had the same
right to live in any American state as anyone born on
the mainland.

The big migration made a new problem out of the
status of Spanish as a foreign language. In New
Mexico, as a carry-over from the time it was a part
of Mexico, Spanish is still a legal language in the
courts and the Legislature. In actuality, English is
almost invariably spoken. An effort to have Spanish
recognized as a native language was made in New York
City not long ago. A lawsuit was filed against the
Board of Electors contending that the municipality
had no legal right to classify Spanish as a foreign
language. The literacy test in English, required of

new voters, was opposed on the basis that Spanish, as the language of Puerto Rico, is automatically a national language of the United States, as well. The test failed, but the issue has not been dropped. Indeed, it was given nationwide attention in March, 1960, when Southern Senators hurled the charge at New York legislators that several hundred thousand Puerto Ricans were being disenfranchised because they could not read or write English.

The status of Puerto Rico as American soil also brought up the question whether the Spanish press on the mainland could properly be referred to as a foreign-language press. The contention was that as Spanish is not an alien tongue in Puerto Rico, it cannot be classified as such on the mainland.

Spanish undoubtedly is the most deeply rooted of all the European minority languages. This reflects half a millenium of Spanish contact with the New World. All of Mexico and most of Central and South America speak it.

Three Spanish dailies and 10 weeklies include at least some English. The bilingual dailies are: the Laredo Times, founded in 1881, 16,000 circulation, El Heraldo de Brownsville, started in 1892, claiming 13,000, both of Texas, and Diario Las Americas (Diary of the Americas), of Miami Springs, Fla., begun in 1954, 17,000.

One of the bilingual weeklies is the Taos News, an English-language newspaper in the New Mexican town of that name until its merger in early March, 1960, with the bilingual El Crepusculo de la Libertad (The Dawn of Liberty). The two names were used to-gether for several issues, until the management found out it could not continue doing so "without violating postal regulations or wading through reams of red tape." So the historic Spanish title was officially dropped, with only a lame reference made to it on the editorial page as: "The Taos News (Combined with El Crepusculo)."

The vicissitudes of these old papers, all weeklies, are exemplified by its experience. Significantly showing the language trend, only one page out of its usual issue of 12 to 14 pages is in Spanish. Even so, much of the advertising on this page is in English.

A paper called El Crepusculo de la Libertad was published four times in 1835 by Padre Martinez, a priest of Taos, 50 miles north of Sante Fe, when the region was a province of Mexico. He used a press on which he printed books for a school he had started. What came next is in doubt, although political organs appeared in the 80s and 90s.

A paper called La Revista de Popular (Popular Review) was begun in Spanish in 1901, and in 1910 its management also put out an English paper called Tao Valley News. Both continued until 1939. The bilingual Taoseno was launched later the same year by new proprietors. After another change in ownership, the paper was bought on August 7, 1948, by E. C. Cabot, of the Boston family, who changed the name to the original El Crepusculo. He leased out the paper, and on its merger, retained part control and contributed an editorial-page column in English.

Thirteen years before El Crepusculo, in 1813, publication was begun at Nacogdoches, Tex., of a paper called Gaceta de Texas (Texas Gazette). The only issue known, a single folio sheet dated May 25, 1813, is marked Vol. 1, No. 1. A Philadelphia printer, Aaron Mowrer, started it with Jose Alvarez de Toledo and William Shaler as editors. The "History and Biography of American Newspapers," by Clarence Saunders Brigham, sponsored by the American Antiquarian Society at Worcester, Mass., declares they published it "to further their side of a political quarrel." Various factions were bitterly competing in the drive for Texan independence. The situation became too hot for the staff, and all three fled 100 miles east to Natchitoches, La., taking along part of the next issue already set in type. The Texas dateline was retained when the paper appeared, although the type-setting was completed and the actual printing done in Louisiana.

Then the trio began a bilingual paper, also one folio sheet, called El Mexicano (The Mexican), the only known issue of which is dated June 19, 1813, marked Vol. 1, No. 2. This indicates that it was considered the continuation of the Gaceta de Texas.

Technically, this paper can claim to be the first published in Texas, or even west of the Mississippi. If its shaky career makes this claim weak, El Crepusculo falls heir to it, although it, too, was short-lived until resurrected in name.

Another bilingual weekly, El Nuevo Mexicano (The New Mexican), of Sante Fe, N. Mex., started in 1849, only a year after Mexico gave up the province to the United States; this was a formality only, as we had taken de facto possession a few years before.

El Espectador (Spectator), a Pomono, Cal., bilingual weekly that began in 1945, claims 8,000 circulation. Another bilingual weekly, La Geceta (The Gazette), of Tampa, Fla., also publishes one page in Italian. It began in 1922, and has above 5,000 circulation. La Verdad (Truth), of Corpus Christi, Tex., is a bilingual that began in 1942, and has 4,000 circulation. The biggest weekly, also bilingual, is La Prensa (The Press), of San Antonio, Tex., started in 1913, with 12,500 circulation.

The pattern for English in foreign-language papers generally ranges from half the paper or maybe one page to a single feature, perhaps a first-page column, an editorial or just several articles.

Two small weeklies are put out entirely in English for Spanish Americans, the Duval County Facts, of San Diego, Tex., and the Tampa Interbay News, in Florida.

The Spanish-speaking American remains attached to his language longer than any other European nationality group. One journalist of Puerto Rican background, speaking fine English, gave me a reason, his eyes glowing. "Spanish is a family language, of sentiment, soft instead of harsh, with a tender effect," he said. "Spanish is like a song that lingers."

Curiously, Spanish was one of the last languages to have a daily in the United States, waiting until 1912, when La Prensa was started in New York City. Twenty-three other languages were already represented by dailies, including Japanese, Chinese and Arabic!

The biggest circulating Spanish daily, El Diario, caters almost exclusively to its big market in New York City, the Puerto Ricans. In the manner of metropolitan journalism, it depends almost entirely on street sales. The paper was near extinction, suspended because of a strike, when resuscitated by adventure-

some, Brooklyn-born Stanley Ross, who switched into
Spanish-language journalism while in South America
as a correspondent for the Associated Press.

Mr. Ross already had edited newspapers in Central
and South America, and had been a reporter and a
"newspaper doctor" in the United States. He had as
"patients" eight papers including the Amsterdam
News, a Negro weekly in New York, when its circulation fell off drastically at the end of the war. One of
Mr. Ross' techniques is to fit the news to his potential
readership. He won't wait for stories to come up, but
stimulates them into being. He studied the colored
community and saw that it was developing its own
social set. So he arranged Negro coming-out parties
for debutantes, then sent a reporter to cover them as
social events. This kind of sympathetic, personal attention started circulation climbing again.

Mr. Ross had learned the distinguishing traits of
the various peoples south of the border, and knew
that beneath the surface similarity in language lay
many subtle differences. He made El Diario reflect the
mind of the Puerto Ricans. He focussed on them as the
only Spanish-speaking group large enough to provide
a healthy circulation.

The typical Puerto Rican had already absorbed the
lushness of the tropics by the time he came under the
American flag. Under United States colonial rule, he
began to look on "government," and especially on our
police force, in a way opposite to the European. The
American mainlander brought friendly, humane institutions in the Yanqui manner, and the Puerto Rican
learned to turn naturally to a government official or
a police officer, without bitterness or fear, for guid-

ance and help in settling his difficulties, even family squabbles that threatened to fly out of hand.

When the Puerto Rican came to the mainland, this contact was cut. The language difference put a barrier between him and those he had been accustomed to rely upon. This was the symbol that Mr. Ross determined to give El Diario. He arranged all sorts of functions that welfare groups and legal aid societies ordinarily fulfill, and even staged a weekly sports program. All this was in Spanish. He made sure, too, that these activities were widely publicized.

Everybody began talking about El Diario. Meanwhile, he filled his pages with the most sensational copy seen in New York City since the English-language tabloid, The Graphic, modified for the Puerto Rican character. His editorials were as controversial and as likely to play havoc with details as did the daily gossip in a sun-charged Puerto Rican village. He caught, in picture and in print, the Puerto Rican type come across in the "San Juan Cannonball," as Manhattan's East Side subway came to be called, or on one of the streets in a Puerto Rican section of the metropolis on a hot afternoon. Fellows in flippant, tight suits and gals in flowing, florid prints, everybody chattering excitedly at once with quick, birdlike sounds that certainly were not the soft and pretty Spanish of Madrid. These were people as disorderly as the jungle, who brought its steamy storms along with them. No immigrant group had ever been like this. Of course, this did not portray the elite minority, but Mr. Ross knew there were not enough of these to feed a hungry circulation. He now has nearly 60,000 daily and almost as much on Sunday.

His principal competitor is La Prensa, the first Spanish-language daily in the United States, which has a solid circulation of 12,000, largely catering to long-time, Spanish-speaking Americans, some located in old communities in the West. Their interests are a world apart from those who arrived only recently. La Pensa is a tabloid newspaper with the same lurid first page that the N. Y. Daily News made the vogue—all picture and headline—but even so, there is little meeting ground inside the paper for the old subscriber and the new. La Prensa seemed to have no alternative but to remain much as it was, or abandon its staid subscribers for the problematical new. It manages to run a fair proportion of world news. Articles about Spain receive ample space, although no Spanish-language paper in the United States is orientated toward Spain politically, only lethargically, for the lingering culture of its past generations.

One phenomenon, exclusive with the Puerto Rican among all arrivals, is that his is the only immigration —or migration—with an ebb and flow to it. A steady although much smaller emigration of Puerto Ricans takes place each year from cold-blooded, wealthy Manhattan island back to their warm-blooded, poor island. The trip by air takes a few hours and is paid for by barely a week's wages. This is a spontaneous movement, not to be compared to the seasonal employment of Mexican farm laborers in the West, arranged and organized by the two governments, with their return stipulated by treaty.

The Puerto Rican, first of all, is interested in what is happening around him, next in Central America, then only and quite superficially in South America, and as for Spain, that's past the horizon of his main cares. So this is how El Diario appraises news values.

Where does this put the United States? The Puerto Rican within the compass of El Diario's newsstands knows he belongs to the United States, but is interested mainly in his own neighborhood, now New York City, in much the way that he used to listen to village gossip. Mr. Ross sagely sized up this Puerto Rican, decided he was no longer mostly interested in news about his island birthplace, but much more so in the local scene where he now lived, activities in the big New York community. So he gave plenty of space and a heavy play to this. He doesn't ignore world news, but tries to cover it in capsule form, rarely running more than four or five international wire stories in any issue, plus the summary of world events.

His judgment was put to a test by El Imparcial, an important newspaper of San Juan, the Puerto Rican capital, that published in New York, too. The New York paper was full of news about "back home" in Puerto Rico, as if Gotham and the mainland weren't home now. The edition ran for a couple of years, reaching a daily circulation of 13,000, but it wasn't enough. After heavy financial loss, it closed shop in New York in September, 1959, and now flies up its Puerto Rico paper for such street sales as can be obtained this way. The quick hop makes this economical.

The business editor of one Spanish-language paper told me that he goes on the assumption that the Spanish-language press caters to a potential clientele of 6,000,000 in the United States, counting first and second generations. Unlike other groups, he said that Spanish remains the language of the second generation, too, and only in the third generation does a tapering off begin. However, there are few of these, if one excludes the old settlers from Spain. Obviously, only a small fraction of these 6,000,000 reads the Spanish-language papers. Most must find that the English-language press satisfied their needs.

The Spaniards came to the New World very early, developing their own pioneer communities, and see little reason to be absorbed by later arrivals. They possess pride of ancestry, tracing their families directly to Spain. The arrivals from Latin America are the newcomers. Spanish still is spoken in New Mexico, Arizona and parts of Texas even by fourth and fifth generation Americans.

The immensity of the sudden Puerto Rican influx has made its absorption difficult, too, particularly considering the strong pull that the Spanish language has on its people.

Continued use of a foreign language slows up assimilation of a new culture, and can even block it. Present-day Spanish-speaking arrivals are under much less pressure to change over to English than was felt by previous immigrant groups. New York City's Spanish-speaking community is self-contained, with a billion-dollar annual income and twenty-eight Spanish theaters. The need to change to English is greatly lessened. Spanish-language papers consequently make practically no effort to encourage the study of English. As the Puerto Rican-born editor said to me, "When one of our young men takes one of our girls to a show, she doesn't like it if it isn't to one of the Spanish theaters."

The question arises whether a saturation point doesn't exist in language absorption, and whether it may not also be found in the acquisition of character traits that are recognized as typically American. The classroom has been our main Americanizing influence, as it receives the second generation of all nationality groups. The Puerto Rican child who goes home hears only Spanish, and then when he goes out to the street to play, it's practically all he hears, too. This has given rise to boyhood gangs along language lines, something New York had not previously experienced.

The lack of a daily among the many Spanish-language newspapers until the eve of World War I is attributed to the turmoil that marked the Spanish American scene. Papers usually belonged to what is known as the junta press. These were weeklies set up as the mouthpiece of some revolutionary or counter-revolutionary faction. Some attained fame, when not notoriety. Jose Marti, Cuban apostle of freedom, while consul in New York for several South American countries, published a weekly, La Patria (The Nation), dedicated to Cuba's emancipation. He had intimate ties, too, with a number of revolutionary weeklies put out in Florida in Spanish to further the Cuban independence movement. Cuba's freedom is indelibly linked with Florida, especially Key West and Tampa, where Marti founded the Cuban Revolutionary Party, and obtained much of his financing. The junta press was an important factor in maintaining enthusiasm at a high pitch. The American officials either looked the other way or they interpreted the law in such a manner as to allow Florida to become the base for

Cuba's liberation, which was necessary for it to suc-
ceed. Spanish-language publications in Florida still
focus on news of nearby Cuba.

A Spanish-language weekly, El Telegrafo de las
Floridas, was printed in 1817 at Fernandina Beach,
on Amelia Island, just below the present Georgia state
line. While expressing deep contempt for Spain, it
announced the establishment of a republican government, and had much to say in support of the Republic
of Florida!

The junta papers generally engaged in clandestine
intrigue and even yet are not strangers to violence and
assassination. Andres Requina, part-time staff writer for El Diario, and bitter opponent of the Trujillo
family regime in the Dominican Republic, made a
date to meet somebody in Harlem. When he alighted
from his taxi and walked into an alley, he was shot
dead. A mistake ended the life of another man named
Bencosne, who answered a doorbell while shaving,
the lather still on his face. Bullets intended for his
roommate, still another Trujillo press enemy, mowed
him down.

Among the Spanish-language papers, La Opinion,
which started in 1926 and has 13,000 circulation
daily, 15,000 Sunday, drums up advertising by making
a novel offer in combination with a Chinese and a
Japanese paper, all in Los Angeles, of a special rate
for simultaneous inclusion. The advertiser knows he
is not duplicating any circulation!

Another daily is El Continental, of El Paso, begun
in 1926, 3,500 circulation.

A striking phenomenon in the Spanish-language
field is the sector published in the United States al-

though not put on sale here, or only incidentally, but sent to Central and South America. These periodicals, published in New York and Chicago, have no parallel in any other language field except for a few in Portuguese for Brazil. None are newspapers, but include newsmagazines.

The bi-weekly newsmagazine Vision, published in Spanish in New York City for export, has more than 100,000 circulation. Its Portuguese edition, Visao, distributes half as many in Brazil. Life, the pictorial newsmagazine, has a bi-weekly Spanish-language counterpart with 350,000 circulation in Latin America. Time magazine and Reader's Digest print their foreign-language editions abroad, wherever possible in the area of distribution.

The advantage of editing and publishing in the United States are threefold. Simultaneous shipment to a large number of countries is faster and more economical, superior printing facilities are available, and press freedom facilitates all-around coverage.

Industrial and professional magazines also are a lucrative field for Spanish-language publications intended mainly for export. These 1958 circulations illustrate the wide scope of these specialized publications, all monthlies:

America Clinica, a journal of medicine, 76,218 circulation; the bilingual American Exporter's Automotive World, 22,064; El Automovil Americano (American Auto), 21,599; El Exportador Americano (American Exporter), 17,155; El Farmaceutico (The Druggist), 13,000, and Guia (Guide), on trade, 20,049.

Chapter Four

The German Pendulum

1. STRENGTH TO WEAKNESS

The German-language press in the United States has the most history back of it. Benjamin Franklin put out a German-language paper on May 6, 1732, simply to help keep his printshop busy. He recognized the big potential market. Having no German in his employ, he entrusted the job to a French journeyman printer, whose German was good, but not that good. The German community would have little to do with the Philadelphische Zeitung, as it was called, and the venture failed after a couple of issues, lasting just long enough to give Franklin another first for his record.

The German-language press effectively began on August 20, 1739 with the publication by Christopher Saur of a newspaper which he modestly entitled "Der Hoch-Deutscher Pennsylvanischer Geschichtsschreiber oder Sammlung der wichtiger Nachrickten aus dem Natu und Kirchenreich."

This means: "The High-German Historian, or Collection of Important News From the Kingdoms of Nature and the Church."

Saur, born in the Palatinate, was raised to be a tailor, but went to America when thirty years old to be a farmer and deal in herbs, but soon showed his versatility by switching to the repair of clocks. He

started printing books in 1738, for which he manu-
factured his own paper and ink and built his own
press. His newspaper caught on, first as a monthly
and then as a weekly, now and then dropping bits of
its meandering title, until it became just Germantauner
Zeitung. As a portent of the catastrophic ordeal that
our wars were to deal the German-language press,
Saur's paper took the wrong side in the Revolution,
which wrecked both it and the family fortunes. It
lasted forty years.

The German press was very much alive during
the colonial and revolutionary years. Five fairly successful papers were published in Pennsylvania during
the latter period. Thirty-eight are recorded in Pennsylvania up to the end of the Eighteenth Century,
14 in 1808. The first news of the adoption of the
Declaration of Independence was printed in a German
paper on July 5, 1776. This was probably the greatest
"scoop" of all time!

The longevity record for consistent publication by
foreign-language dailies in the United States is held
by a German paper, the New Yorker Staats-Zeitung
und Herold (New York State Journal and Herald),
born 126 years ago on Christmas Eve, 1834. From its
start until the last few decades, it took deep draughts
of politics. Its first editor was a theology student from
Silesia named Adolph Neumann, who insisted that it
be an American paper expressing German culture
and preserving the German language. Although it
started as a weekly, it became a daily within its first
year of publication.

The German press all along has maintained high
professional standards. Until the post-World War

II period, it never hesitated to plunge into the deepest waters of political controversy. The German-language press of today, with club news filling the space that editorial matter formerly occupied, is a far cry from the outspoken papers of its past. Many German editors, including outstanding ones, were political refugees. Once on American soil, they drank deep of the heady wine of a free press, and jumped heavily and boldly into the political ring.

Immigration during all these years had to provide not only readers for the foreign-language newspapers, but their editors and staff. These writers had to learn about America by experience, too, and what they learned they passed on to their readers, each paper reflecting the character of its publisher and staff, creating a bond between newspaper and subscriber that made for intimate, personal journalism which lingers on to this day in the foreign-language field.

The foreign-language paper replaced relatives and friends left behind in the "old country." This gave a great impetus to personal journalism, that alone can develop the initiative which made our early press a great influence.

The 1848 Revolution in Germany fired the German population in the United States with enthusiasm. On its collapse, many of its participants fled to America to continue the struggle, greatly adding to the ranks of liberal-minded Germans in the United States, and radical-minded ones, too.

Hundreds of political refugees came with this new wave of German immigrants. Included were men of the highest talent. They joined German staffs or started papers of their own.

With indomitable optimism they gave America their message that had been suppressed in Germany, starting in at once to inculcate readers and associates with their new ideas. The German communities hungrily drank in their words, eager to learn the latest, most controversial thinking in Europe. The impact of this early liberalism on the American scene is incalculable.

American politicians, not slow to note this influence, determined to reach the large German-speaking population, too, through the numerous papers that served its communities across the country. The German editor in this way won recognition and respect outside his community, enabling the German-born population as a whole to exert its power and to win many favors.

The German press reached its peak in prestige and influence in the ante-bellum years up to the Civil War. The issue of unrestricted immigration first arose during those years. The Germans and the Irish were arriving in such large numbers that alarm was expressed that the character of the United States was being fundamentally changed. The fervor with which the radical editors who had fled from Germany turned their attention to thoroughly making over America, from its eating habits and art to its business methods and political system, left little room for existing customs. The air of superiority with which this was propagated was resented as arrogance. Such factors, as usual, led to extremism. A so-called nativist movement arose, with hate and violence close behind. Undaunted, the German press took the leadership of all the minority elements for the counter-attack.

In the elections of the 1850s and 1860s, all political parties recognized the perhaps decisive importance of the foreign vote. This gave unparalleled prestige to the German press. The liberalizing mood that characterized its refugee editors saw in the slavery issue a wholly American problem to which they could transfer their frustrated cravings for reform in Germany, and they opposed slavery with all their revived vigor. Almost unanimously they fought against its extension into additional states.

On another reform measure—prohibition—the German-language press also was virtually united, this time on the negative side. The German was unable to visualize any kind of social life unaccompanied by schnapps. This determined his entire thinking on the liquor question. The German press was on the side of beer, and a whisper of any other view would have brought its German readers storming into the editorial sanctums faster than any other issue. They easily saw in this not the proclaimed reform, but deprivation of personal liberties that would surely exact terrible penalties by corroding the American respect for freedom within the law.

The German press and its readers, all during this period, while stubbornly insisting on autonomy for their language and culture, showed little interest in Europe, less than that of any other immigrant group. Even the first generation became immersed in their new surroundings and opportunities, enthusing over their adopted country. The second-generation German did so almost utterly.

Then came Bismarck and his war with France in 1870. When the German armies swept the supposedly invincible French Army before them all the way to the grand capital at Paris, in the blitzkreig of that day, the attention of the world was galvanized. The Germans in America caught the fever.

This episode and its tragic significance are explained by the educator, Carl Wittke, in his detailed study, "The German-Language Press in America." The intense pride that had been reserved for the culture of Germany was shifted to the German state and government. The beneficiary of this new admiration by the predominantly liberal German element in America, through a strange twist in history, was the Hohenzollern empire.

Only one German-language daily, the Staats-Zeitung, has been able to survive in New York City. Its formula is a skillful balance of general news with a thorough and personal coverage of personalities and activities in the numerous clubs and societies that make up the German-speaking community. The latter is its bread and butter. Its balding, shirt-sleeved managing editor, Dr. Ludwig Oberndorf, was a newspaperman in Germany before he came to the United States in 1913. He first worked a year with the Gazette-Democrat of Philadelphia, a weekly started in 1838, of 4,000 circulation, now being put out by New York City's Staats-Zeitung. He then joined the latter paper, making it his career. In his nearly half a century with it, he has witnessed what he frankly calls a shocking decline in the German-language press.

When he began, 800 to 900 newspapers, magazines and other periodicals were being published in German,

including 80 to 90 dailies, more than the present total
in all the foreign languages. While there are only
three dailies left in German, 33 German-language
papers, including seven bilingual, appear weekly, one
semi-weekly and one tri-weekly. Of the weeklies, two
are religious in content and one partly so.

A striking feature of the German minority press
is its big religious weeklies entirely in English, published by German Christian groups. The Lutheran
Standard of Columbus, Ohio, appearing since 1943,
has 143,000 circulation, and the glossy, magazine-
sized The Lutheran, of Philadelphia, in existence since
1918, 192,000. Others are the Gospel-Herald, put out
by the Mennonites in Scottsdale, Pa., since 1908,
18,000, and The Mennonite, of Newton, Kan., 15,000.
The United Brethren in Christ puts out the United
Brethren at Huntington, Ind., 8,500.

One of the hardest-hitting, anti-communist papers
in America is The Wanderer, a full-sized newspaper of
usually eight pages, that appears as a national Catholic weekly at St. Paul, Minn., 10,000 circulation. The
Wanderer only a few years ago changed over from
German, in which it had been publishing since 1867.
Its lengthy editorials deal with topical subjects.

The two strictly news bilingual weeklies are: Troy
Freie Presse (Troy Free Press), of Troy, N. Y.,
started in 1870, 3,000 circulation, and the New Braunsfels Zeitung-Chronicle, of New Braunsfels, S. Dak.,
dating back to 1852, 6,000.

The Swiss Americans have two weeklies in America.
They are: Amerikanische Schweizer Zeitung (American Swiss Gazette), of New York City, which began
in 1868, a little above 4,000 circulation, and the Swiss

Journal (Schweizer-Journal), started 1918, 2,000 circulation, that also prints occasional items in Italian. The Siebenbuergisch - Amerikanisches Volksblatt (Transylvania-American People's Journal), publishing in Detroit since 1905, has 4,000 circulation.

The German-language papers try to make themselves indispensable by providing a service unobtainable in the English-language press. They keep their readers in close touch with the numerous German American clubs and societies. The typical English-language, smalltown paper particularly near a big city, that fills its pages with local items for which its overpowering competitor has no space, is doing the same thing.

One of the outstanding German-language editors told me that about half of America's population has at least some German blood. I saw no need to check up, for there is no doubt that an important percentage of Americans are of more or less some German descent. Whatever the figure, it was dramatic evidence of the phenomenal strength of the American way of life—our melting pot—in taking hold of the alien at one end of the immigration process, and within observable time, turning out a truly Americanized citizen. The exceptions are few enough to prove the rule.

The German dailies appear in New York City, Chicago and Rochester, N. Y., the last-named because its printshop publishes weeklies as well, one for New York City. The Rochester Abendpost (Rochester Evening Post) was started in 1851, and has 13,678 circulation. Wittke writes, regarding the Nazi period:

"Papers like the New Yorker Staats-Zeitung und Herold and the Rochester Abendpost were embarrassed and disturbed by developments in Germany. They tried as far as possible to avoid the issues, while maintaining an essentially American isolationist policy in which the old anti-British note was a factor. Other German papers, like the Florida Echo of Miami, the Schenectady Herold-Journal, the Gross Daytoner Zeitung, and the Catholic German weekly of Omaha, were definitely anti-Nazi and the Neue Volkszeitung, a Social-Democratic weekly of New York, was violently so."

The Staats-Zeitung has 21,000 daily and 38,000 Sunday circulation. The Abendpost und Milwaukee Deutsche Zeitung (Evening Post and Milwaukee German Press), and the Sonntagpost und Milwaukee Deutsche Zeitung (Sunday Post), its Sunday edition, of Chicago, both of which began in 1889, have 27,000 and 30,000 circulation respectively. There is no Saturday paper.

The Detroiter Abend-Post (Detroit Evening Post), a tri-weekly that goes back to 1854, has 5,500 circulation. The American Herold und Lincoln Freie Presse (American-Herald and Lincoln Free Press) and its companion, Sonntagspost (Sunday Post), of Winona, Minn., going back to 1873, have 10,500 and 10,000 circulation respectively. The former appears Wednesday and the latter Sunday.

The other general news weeklies have about 5,000 circulation to a thousand or so. They obviously are hanging on by the skin of their teeth.

The vast German immigration came between 1880 and 1890, sometimes a million persons a year. Most stayed for a longer or shorter period in New York. How could circulation then be any problem? The typical present-day alien from Germany has already read English papers in Europe. They arrive Americanized to a degree, due to the occupation, but this will not end when the Americans withdraw, as English is being taught in West German schools from the sixth grade on. Not many Germans are coming, as they are not pressed to emigrate by economic reasons any longer; there is 100 per cent employment, and the government of Konrad Adenauer is encouraging the young to stay at home.

The statistics must be seen to grasp the tremendously wide scope of the German-language press before its debacle. In 1874 there were 58 dailies, 74 in 1876, 82 in 1883, and still 78 in 1904, besides hundreds of other German periodicals. When this is compared to the vast increase in population since then, these figures become immensely more impressive.

The main vulnerability of the German press, as well as that of the other foreign-language papers, was their dependence on immigration. Although 8,282,618 persons gave Germany as their country of origin in the 1910 census, half had been born in the United States of German parents, and another million and a half were born here with one German parent. Only two and a half million were really first generation. All their lifetime, the rest had felt the influence of the American environment, if only at school or on the job, no matter how Germanic their home and club.

They were American, not German, when the chips were down, as was proven in two wars.

The German-language press actually had grown too big for its britches; the number of papers being published were economically out of balance with their circulation and advertising potential. With the peak attained, rationalization was already beginning with consolidation and elimination of some of the smaller sheets. This process had already been going on for several decades when the big blow struck from which the German-language press never recovered. Indeed, before it could regain its equilibrium it was dealt another, similar punch. These were the blows dealt by World Wars I and II.

The sympathy of the German-language press with the Entente in World War I and with the Axis in World War II, until the United States entered the fray, is well enough known not to require re-telling here. The ugly aspects of Hitler's subversive reach into newspaper offices is "old stuff" now, but the scars have not all been removed from many memories. Suffice it to point out that with the entry of the United States into each war, the German-language press as a whole—the portion of it, at least, that survived— fulfilled its duty as essentially an American press written in German. In this, it reflected the sentiments of its readers.

The patriotic conduct of the American in whom flowed a generous portion of German blood was one of the most inspiring stories in American history, a justification of the American ideal, opposed by the atavistic concept that put tribal limits to nationality.

But the German American, nonetheless, went through a purgatory in World War I that left his minority press only a fraction of what it had been. While World War II was less severe on him, it further shattered the German-language press. The German press totaled 40 per cent of the 1,300 foreign-language papers and periodicals in 1914, with one-third of the dailies, or 53 in German, five in New York. It still also led in subscribers. Wartime circulation was soaring on all newspapers, and so it was with the German.

The chauvinism which had seen its birth in Bismarck's startling victories had swollen with the Kaiser's egomania. Alongside it all else suddenly became as if inconsequential. Fed by an historic distrust of Great Britain, virtual hysteria rose as the war progressed, with the United States coming closer and closer to actual involvement. Once we were in, the hysteria embraced all sides. Anything German in blood or culture, from a person's own name to a song, including the German-language press, became automatically more than suspect. Only at his own peril did a reader now receive his German-language newspaper in his postbox, or be seen buying it.

"It need hardly be added that the spearhead of such demonstrations (mob violence) was almost always directed against the German-language press," Wittke writes. "Not only had the press been outspokenly pro-German before 1917, but it was the greatest cohesive force which held the German group together. Publishers of German-language papers made every effort to satisfy their critics. They printed the Star-Spangled Banner on the front pages of Fourth

of July issues, urged their readers to memorize the
national anthem, decorated their papers with American flags, and pleaded with readers to fulfill their
obligations as United States citizens. The German
press furnished advertising space free of charge for
various patriotic causes, published official information, and printed the testimony of high government
officials concerning its loyal public service. Never-
theless, German-American journalists continued to
tread a path of thorns."

Circulation took as great a dive when we entered
the war as it had risen since hostilities began, then
continued dropping. Loss of advertising, however,
and not circulation, sounded the death knell for most
of the German-language papers. All too late, the
German-language press had changed its tune. Not all
at once, but within a few months, at most. Cynical
opinions were expressed of this volte face, but it
was no less sincere than that of German-language
subscribers, who, now that their adopted country had
irrevocably come to a decision, went along with it,
in agony certainly. America's own hesitancy had en-
trapped them. They had been led into opposing American policy through opposition to London and not
Washington at a time when the former was at war
and we were not. More serious was their failure,
considering the policies first of the Kaiser's government and then of Hitler's, to see the basic conflict
and hence the inevitable clash with the American way
of life.

In 1920, after World War I, only 26 German dailies
were left, and 278 German periodicals, mostly small

religious, club and trade publications. The heart had been taken out of the German-language press. In contrast to its former vitality, it was now inclined to avoid editorializing or taking sides, content to replace opinion with club news and social items.

The Nazi period dealt a new blow to the German press, both by the mesmerism of Hitler's rantings and the lack of immigrant replacements for circulation lost to the English-language press. Refugees from Germany were educated and able to read English, and especially when Jewish, had no wish to remind themselves of the hell they had left by reading what the German-language papers contained. As for the editors themselves, once bitten, they were twice shy, but with a few notable exceptions, not sufficiently so to take an anti-Nazi stand. They took refuge in isolationism while still fiercely anti-British. Once again, they were caught in a trap set by historic consequences. Their press continued its decline, hastened now by the trend toward mergers in the American press generally. Of all the German publications remaining in the United States in 1956, Wittke writes: "Hardly more than two dozen could be described as newspapers."

Herr Oberndorf, seated at his corner desk in the upstairs newsroom of the modest, modern plant occupied by the Staats-Zeitung on the Long Island side of New York City, close enough to La Guardia international airport to hear the planes beat a regular tattoo in the skies, philosophically explained how the two World Wars differed in their effect.

"German-Americans were persecuted in World War I, afraid to be seen with a German-language paper," he said. "If delivered to an apartment building and others saw it, there was trouble. We lost nearly half our circulation this way. Anything in German was taboo; the language wasn't taught. In World War II the government acted the opposite. We taught our soldiers to speak German, and the government put out propaganda in German. The German language was taught in school. Even this was not the major difference. Instead of it being a problem of relationship with the United States public or the government that created our difficulties, it was the ideological split among the German Americans themselves.

"We of the Staats-Zeitung were considered Nazis by the Jews and Jews by the Nazis!"

German editors are now confronted with the task of giving its spirit back to the German-language press in a context befitting the new times. Little effort to do so can be discerned. Maybe the shadow of World War III is too close. How tragic it would be, after the German-language press twice had been disastrously tripped up, if it were to be beguiled now into excessive caution on world issues when a vigorous policy reminiscent of the editors of the post-1848 period would bring the German press into harmony with the true interests of America, and of Germany too.

2. SOME OUTSTANDING FAMILIES

A number of America's outstanding publishing families and editors have more or less of a German background. Joseph Pulitzer grew up in Budapest.

His fiery, Magyar temperament was never much beneath the surface. He tried to get into the Austrian Army, French Foreign Legion and British military, but his poor sight and less than husky physique prevented it. He finally signed up with a recruiting agent at Hamburg for the Union Army, and went to Boston in 1864. He joined the First New York (Lincoln) Cavalry, organized by Carl Schurz, who was then a major general. Most of its members were Germans. After demobilization, he ultimately became a reporter on the Westliche Post in St. Louis, owned by Carl Schurz. He was elected to the Missouri Lower House in 1869, but was ineligible because of his youth. He attended anyway, as correspondent for his paper. He became part owner in 1871, disposing of his interests two years later.

He bought the St. Louis Staats-Zeitung for a song, then made a big profit selling its Associated Press franchise for $200,000. In 1878 he bought the St. Louis Dispatch, and with its A. P. franchise, negotiated a merger with the St. Louis Post. The St. Louis Post-Dispatch is the only newspaper property the family still owns. In 1883, Pulitzer bought The World in New York from Jay Gould, and founded the Evening World in 1887.

The Ochs family, that built up the N. Y. Times, came from Bavaria. Julius Ochs, apprenticed to a bookbinder, walked 600 miles to Bremen to emigrate to America in 1845. His son, Adolph S., acquired the Chattanooga Times in 1878, when he was 20, and made his father treasurer. In 1896 be bought the N. Y. Times, making his younger brother, George

Washington Ochs, general manager of the Chattanooga paper. The latter changed his name by court procedure in 1917, taking the family name of Oaks, in bitterness over Germany's military madness.

The Villards of the old N. Y. Evening Post and the Nation—when those publications were very different in character—were from Bavaria, too. A young man named Ferdinand Heinrich Gustav Hilgard approved of the leadership taken by his two uncles in the 1848 Revolution in Rhenish Bavaria, and in an argument over it with his father, left home and emigrated to America in 1853.

Fearing he might be traced and returned to Europe, he changed his name to Henry Villard. His great love became journalism, but his new name became known worldwide as that of America's greatest railway speculator. He gained control of the Northern Pacific by what became known as "blind pool". He offered a share in the new exploit to a select few who were allowed to contribute some millions of dollars each to it, without being told its nature.

His first couple of years in the U. S. were spent reading law, peddling books, selling real estate—and editing a smalltown paper. He became special correspondent for the Staats-Zeitung of New York in 1858, reporting the Lincoln-Douglas debates. He went to Pike's Peak county in 1859 at the time of the gold rush, as correspondent for the Cincinnati Commercial. He soon was correspondent for a number of New York newspapers. When the Civil War erupted, he became correspondent for the N. Y. Herald, and later for the N. Y. Tribune. At the Staats-Zeitung, they say he also sent them war dispatches.

With the wealth acquired by his financial wizardry, he was able to put his ideas in journalism into practice. These boiled down into one; the acquisition of as highly talented a group of editors as possible, with unquestioned integrity, and turning the paper over to them to run. He did so, buying the Evening Post, bringing in Carl Schurz, E. L. Godkin and Horace White to determine editorial policy, and abdicating his own control of it. His belief in an independent and fearless press was more than verbal.

William Randolph Hearst, although of Scotch and English forebears, showed his versatility by acquiring the New Yorker Zeitung, but this German-language daily became a World War I casualty.

The name of John Peter Zenger, who came to America from Germany when 13, is indelibly identified with our press freedoms. He launched the New York Weekly Journal in 1733, the first paper started for political reasons. Before it was a year old, Zenger was arrested for seditious libel. He missed only one issue in eight months of imprisonment, editing it all the while. Zenger recognized the great issue at stake. Truth could not be libelous, he insisted, opposing the weight of the entire colonial government. Even to this day, this principle is not accepted in England. He won his case. Gouverneur Morris called the verdict "the morning star of that liberty which subsequently revolutionized America."

No name is more outstanding in its identity with the German-language press than that of Carl Schurz, who became Secretary of the Interior in the Hayes Cabinet. He was famous among the German

Forty-Eighters for his Americanizing influence. This was a life-long career for him. His whole career, too, was identified with German-language papers. He was a member of the Republican National Committee when Lincoln ran for President. The German press played an undeniable, major role in the election, perhaps a decisive one.

Abraham Lincoln, recognizing the importance of the German vote, bought a German newspaper, the Illinois Staatsanzeiger of his home town, paying $400 for it. The editor stayed at his desk to campaign for Lincoln. After the election, Lincoln sold him back his paper, and as a reward for his services, sent him to Vienna as American consul.

Certainly one of the best-known German-language newspaper families was the Ridders. They have now shed themselves of their German-language press connections, switching over completely to building up an English-language newspaper network. Later on they acquired a set of English-language radio and television stations, to go with it.

One of the alert, younger members of the Washington press corps, proud to consider himself a reporter—the mark of a real journalist—is Walter Ridder. His is the fourth generation. He is Washington bureau chief for Ridder Publications, Inc., that consists of eight newspapers including the New York Journal of Commerce, the St. Paul Pioneer Press & Dispatch, the Duluth Herald & News-Tribune, and several radio-TV stations. He covered Nixon's trip to Soviet Russia and Eisenhower's to South America. A "Kitchen Cabinet" certificate is posted on his office wall as a souvenir of the journey to the U.S.S.R.

The founder of the family fortunes was named Herman Ridder, member of a Westphalia farming family. His start is almost lost in legend. One family report says he shipped out as a sailor, and liked the United States so much when his ship put in here in the 1840s that he stayed. Maybe this was his intent all along, for it was a hectic period of revolution in Germany. All agree he had no part in the uprising.

He was every bit a family man, raising eleven children. The eldest was Herman, too, who had the instincts of a journalist. He sold insurance to German Catholic institutions, which gave him the idea of starting a German Catholic weekly, which he did in 1886, calling it Volksblatt (People's Journal). About ten years later, after his death, his sons changed it into an English-language weekly, the present-day Catholic News, of New York, still run by the family.

The Staats-Zeitung, during this early period, was owned by Oswald Ottendorfer, who was deep in New York politics as a reform Democrat fighting Tammany. The Ottendorfer branch of the New York Public Library was on of his numerous philanthropies. Herman Ridder became his business manager about 1888, when Offendorfer was a very rich, old man, wracked by age and illness, practically retired. He sold him the paper in a couple of years. The new owner met disaster sometime later in a business venture. He organized the Intertype Company, a competitor of Linotype. His bad break was the outbreak of World War I. Operations were crippled, and he found himself squeezed out, bankrupt and owing a million and more dollars. The firm now is one of the biggest.

His debts could legally have been sidestepped, but his family gradually paid them off.

This repayment gave the Ridders the financial standing, when they heard that the Journal of Commerce was for sale, to be able to buy it. Soon after this purchase, something new was started in American journalism, the tabloid N. Y. Daily News, which desperately needed an Associated Press franchise. The Journal of Commerce had one, and it turned out to be its biggest asset. The Ridders sold it to the Daily News for a tidy sum.

There are so many Ridders in journalism—eleven of them—that no two people seem to agree who's who, and understandably. Herman's three sons, Bernard, Joseph and Victor, the last two twins, operated as a team, each liable overnight to appear at any one of their numerous offices to sit in for the real incumbent. In a first-term appointment, President Roosevelt picked a Ridder, but James A. Farley and Hugh Johnson all had a different idea which Ridder had been selected, and never quite were sure.

The Ridder separation from the German-language field was brought about by several factors. One was the shattering effect of the two World Wars on the German-language press generally. There was the personal factor of the eight sons of the three Ridder brothers. The family was expanding in the old manner, the sons remaining within the fold, the daughters spreading out into other spheres. The Staats-Zeitung certainly could not satisfy them all. Third generation Americans already, they no longer had the same intimate identity with the German language as their elders. The determining factor, however, was the identification in the popular mind of the Ridder name with the German-language field exclusively. So long as they remained in it at all, whatever English-language enterprise they entered would seem subordinate to the German-language interest. Yet the latter was declining with the reduced immigration.

A psychological factor must have entered, too. The Ridders, as owners of the Staats-Zeitung through two great wars, had gone through an unhappy experience. They wanted nothing to remind them of this any more. They sold the paper in 1952. The decks were now cleared for the new generation.

The smoothness with which this transfer was achieved is a tribute to the Ridder sagacity and family unity. Their first purchase was the Long Island Press in Jamaica, New York City, as an experiment to find out whether they could operate successfully in the English-language field. They say they found it much easier than the foreign-language field. From then on, they expanded without hesitancy.

3. THE AMAZING AUFBAU

A survey of the German-language press would be incomplete without specific note being taken of the tabloid weekly newspaper Aufbau (Reconstruction), with its more than 30,000 circulation.

The paper is a product of the German refugee period, when throngs of educated Jews, in contrast to the earlier Jewish peasant immigration from regions such as Poland and the Ukraine, poured into New York City. The existing German-language press did not appeal to them for understandable reasons. Firstly, its general attitude toward the Nazis, when not subtly favorable, was noncommittal. Secondly, its interests seemed far-fetched to the newcomer, for it was focussed on social and business life in the American locale, whereas he was still more concerned about developments in Europe.

Even the writing in the American German-language press had developed some mannerisms. The German-language papers catered to their average reader, and paid little heed to literature and the drama, as these intellectual refugees had known them abroad. Even less did it cover refugee experiences.

A vacuum therefore existed. A broad-minded German, Dr. Wilfred Hulse, who had left the Reich some years before Hitler's rise to power, joined several others in expanding the items in an ordinary four-paged, mimeographed bulletin put out in a mid-Manhatten synagogue by one of its fraternal groups. The response was immediate and extremely encouraging, and they began to circulate it outside as a news weekly.

In a short while, it was on the newsstands, and its growth was consistent from then on. With an expanding circulation, its advertising mounted, making it a financial success, as well.

The influx of refugees who had joined this conveniently-located synagogue and entered its social activities had taken hold of an ordinary weekly bulletin such as most churches put out, and had broadened its horizon bit by bit, until what they had on their hands was no longer a bulletin but a newspaper. Under the influence of the American environment and such men as Dr. Hulse, who from the start saw beyond the small group, Aufbau gained readers among all who were interested in the German refugee and his work.

Now it refers to itself in its masthead as "An American Weekly" published by the New World Club, Inc., and has a fair circulation, too, among Christians of German background, attracted by its special coverage of the drama and literature.

Aufbau celebrated its twenty-fifth birthday on November 8, 1959, at a concert meeting of 3,000 former refugees. Occupying the same platform were the ambassadors of both West Germany and Israeli, and this extraordinary sight was applauded as a token of the new day.

Aufbau had a tremendous advantage from the start. The refugees included world-famous writers who were only too willing to contribute to it, for they were confronted with the agonizing problem of finding an outlet for their work in German.

The editor is Dr. Manfred George, who was brought here as a nearly penniless refugee from Berlin in 1939 to take over the post. He had been the brilliant editor of Tempo, a daily boulevard paper. The advisory board includes Sen. Jacob K. Javits, Roger N. Baldwin and Freda Kirchwey, while its former members include Albert Einstein and Thomas Mann.

Under this sophisticated guidance, Aufbau has become soft toward left extremism, reflecting the hesitancies and confusion on communism in so-called intellectual circles. During the heroic Hungarian uprising against communist enslavement, one would have expected a refugee newspaper to have hailed this

struggle of a stricken European people for freedom.
Aufbau glossed over what is probably this generation's most inspiring event.

As part of its twenty-fifth anniversary, a series
of Franklin D. Roosevelt Awards was presented at
a gala dinner and ball in the Starlight Roof of the
Waldorf Astoria. Mrs. Eleanor Roosevelt received an
award. One looked in vain for any indication of concern for the later refugees who have fled from communist terror in Eastern Europe or Asia. It were as
if totalitarianism meant the twin on the right, not
really the twin to the left.

This is a cul-de-sac into which a great segment of
otherwise liberal-thinking personalities have lost their
way. Aufbau was a stimulant to the refugee from
Hitler in its first quarter of a century. The mark it
leaves in its second quarter-century might very well
be determined by its capacity to broaden its scope once
more, to show a crusading interest in the still captive
peoples, even in East Germany.

Chapter Five

This Group and That

1. THE DRAMATIC ITALIAN

The Italian-language press, which dropped nearly a quarter of a million in the circulation of its various publications since 1942, has followed a dramatic although not always happy course. World War I was beneficial for the Italian-language papers, but World War II was a disaster. The Italian-language press as a whole had fallen for Mussolini's antics, and was still in favor of the Axis when Pearl Harbor brought the United States into the war.

A group of Italians who had been anti-Fascist all along, courageous refugees from totalitarianism, felt that they had now the right to take over the Italian-language press. Carlo Tresca, editor of the relentless anti-Fascist paper, Il Martello, had been shot down and slain on New York City streets. Generoso Pope, who made a fortune in sand, stone and cement, spent part of it on his Il Progresso Italo-Americano (Italian-American Progress), founded in 1880, which now has a daily and Sunday circulation of nearly 70,000. A prominent figure in New York politics, he had once helped a rising politician, Franklin D. Roosevelt, run for Governor. Roosevelt was now President, and Pope appealed to him.

The Chief Executive, who didn't forget political favors, put his weight down and saved the paper for

Pope. Even so, one of the family's Italian dailies collapsed and Il Progresso, which had reached its peak of 160,000 circulation after World War I, promptly lost more than half its remaining readers. They didn't feel it was tactful to be seen reading an Italian paper.

The Italian-language newspapers never recovered. Most second generation Italians turn to English, and the comparatively few immigrants who come buy an Italian paper only as an adjunct to whatever English-language one they regularly read.

The most phenomenal influence of the Italian press has been in raising the prestige of the Italian immigrant. The tone for this was set by a mixed-up emotionalist named Carlo Barsotti, who started Il Progresso in 1879 in a pique because the only existing Italian-language paper then in New York, Eco d'Italia, refused to run his articles protesting against a death sentence imposed on an Italian for merely killing his wife. Barsotti, who started out as a labor gang foreman on the railways, had become a partner in a 25-cent a night flophouse, that brought in so much money that he soon owned a string of them.

With this as his qualification for becoming a newspaper publisher, Barsotti soon made Il Progresso a financial success. Spurred on by this, his next move was to open a bank, which naturally made him more money. Meanwhile, he began using his newspaper for the most successful public relations drive ever conducted on behalf of a foreign-language community, setting out to elevate the standing of Italians in general. The immigrants were mostly unskilled laborers who patiently and conscientiously did the dirty, hard work that a new country needs. They were un-excelled in this. Barsotti wanted the American public to acquire a more lofty conception of the Italian's capacity. He conducted a series of fund-raising campaigns for monuments to Italian explorers and statesmen. These were located at the most dramatic crossings and esplanades on Manhattan island, which were given the names of these great Italian thinkers and heroes.

This was how the colossal Columbus Monument came to be erected at a corner of Central Park, which was named Columbus Circle, how the statue to Guiseppe Garibaldi, the fiery leader who united Italy after saving Uruguay, was put up at Washington Square, in the Bohemian quarter of the city, and how the bust of Giovanni da Verrazano, who discovered the Hudson River before Henry Hudson explored it, was located at the Battery, where it could look out over the majestic entrance to the harbor.

Generoso Pope, after buying Il Progresso, continued the Barsotti pattern by conducting the campaign that made Columbus Day a national holiday, with a tremendous parade in New York City, instead of merely a simple ceremony attended only by Italians, as heretofore. Fortune Pope, when he succeeded to his father's paper, went on from these to conduct the campaign to give da Verrazano's name to the new bridge being built across the Narrows in New York Harbor, which is to have the longest span in the world.

The Italian American press is an intriguing study in the course taken by a major immigrant group in which all the stages of absorption can still be observed, from the comparatively recent arrival to the 100 per cent American who retains anxious interest in the county of his ancestors and a cultural pride in their language.

The four Italian dailies have double the circulation of the three German, and although there are fewer weeklies, the combined circulation of those that carry general news is also far greater. The Italian press has more bilingual papers, too.

The dailies besides Il Progresso, are: La Notizia (News), Boston, 1916, 37,000 excluding Sunday; Il Popolo Italiano (Italian People), Philadelphia, 1935, 15,500 daily and Sunday, and I'Italia (Italy), San Francisco, going back to 1886, 14,500 daily except Monday.

Of 22 Italian weeklies, 15 are bilingual, and almost all are general newspapers. Of the seven all-Italian weeklies, one is the art and literary magazine Divagando (Recreation), 1942, 15,000 circulation, and another is political, L'Adunata dei Refrattari (The Call of the "Refractaires"), 1922, 8,000, both New York City. The circulation of the all-Italian general newsweeklies range between two and six thousand by irregular steps, the highest being L'Italia, a Chicago Sunday paper begun in 1886.

Eight of the 15 bilingual weeklies have 10,000 circulation or above. These are: Sons of Italy Times, Philadelphia, put out since 1936 by the Pennsylvania Grand Lodge of the Order of Sons of Italy in America, 50,000 circulation; La Tribuna Italiana (Italian Tribune), Milwaukee, 1933, 22,000; Italian Tribune, Newark, N. J., 1931, 20,000; L'Unione

(Union), Pittsburgh, 1890, 15,000; La Voce del Popolo (Voice of the People), Detroit, 1910, 14,500; La Tribuna Italiana D'America, also Detroit, 1909, 14,000; Gazzetta del Massachusetts (Massachusetts Gazette), Boston, 1896, 14,000, and La Libera Parole (Free Speech), Philadelphia, 1918, 10,000.

In addition, there are several monthlies, semi-monthlies and bi-monthlies of a more or less general news nature, all bilingual, such as Sentinel Press, a Greensburg, Pa., semi-monthly, 1933, 8,000 circulation, and Il Corriere del Popolo (People's Messenger), a San Francisco monthly, 8,000.

There are also three English-language weeklies for Italian Americans: Italian News, Boston, 1921, 14,000; Texas Tribune, Dallas, 1927, 3,200, and the Colorado, of Denver, 1905, 2,000.

The only Italian paper in Rome is the monthly English-language Rome Tribune, founded in 1914— the Rome in New York State, that is.

First-generation Italians have always been insistent that Italian-language papers give them good coverage of the "old country", but this intense interest drops tremendously with the second generation. As evidence, there were 26 Italian-language papers in New York City alone in 1922, nine others in Philadelphia and nine in San Francisco, eight in Chicago and four in Pittsburgh. Most were weeklies.

Philip M. Rose, in his controversial "The Italians in America", published in 1922, reported 191 dailies and weeklies, mostly the latter, then being published throughout the United States. Italian papers that had the biggest circulation, he wrote, were accepting their "unlimited opportunity" for "a sympathetic presentation of the meaning and ideals of America." He mentioned, too, that ordinary, English-language papers at that time sometimes printed several columns or an entire page in Italian.

2. INCLUDING THE GREEK

A comparative table of foreign-language periodicals of all description, in number and circulation, compiled by the Common Council, gives a picture of the ups and downs, mostly downs, that confront their editors. These periodicals include everything of that nature in the language, which in some cases is not representative of the press generally, certainly not its news side. Sometimes the sort of routine bulletin that a church produces slips into a list. All in all, though, the statistics give an intriguing insight into the field. The 1960 column has been added mainly on the basis of the Council's latest annual Foreign Language Press Lists.

The striking drop in Swedish periodicals from 47 in 1942 to 20 in 1959 and 12 in 1960 is indicative of the evolution generally, as well as in the Scandinavian field. The Norwegian was 37 in 1942, only 17 last year, 12 now. The Danish, with an over-all circulation in 1959 of 25,617, a third of its 1942 total, has dropped from 18 to seven periodicals. The only Swedish general news publication is a weekly, Bien (The Bee), of San Francisco, with 3,000 circulation.

The Norwegian community has a weekly newspaper in existence since 1874 in the small town of Decorah, Iowa, yet it has 18,000 circulation. This is the Posten Og Ved Arnen (Post and Fireside). Five other news weeklies include Nordisk Tidende (Norwegian News), launched 1891, Brooklyn, 9,500 circulation; Minnesota Posten, Minneapolis, 1940, 6,000; Washington Posten, Seattle, 1889, above 4,000; Duluth Skandinav (Duluth Scandinavian), of Minnesota, 1887, 1,250, and Superior Tidende (Superior Time), of Superior, Wisc., founded 1888, struggling along at 125 circulation! Obviously this is a labor of love, for its editor and offices are the same as the Duluth Skandinav, in Duluth.

The table is arranged in order of combined circulations up to spring, 1959, for languages above the 50,000 figure.

Foreign-Language Periodicals in the U. S.

	Circulation		Periodicals		
	1942	1959	1942	1959	1960
Polish	999,202	745,833	78	49	45
German	683,653	554,997	150	72	60
Italian	727,883	492,855	117	55	45
Spanish	395,570	460,679	125	74	52
Jewish	609,853	354,005	50	35	34
Czech	563,616	340,168	61	34	32
Lithuanian	269,527	250,384	27	36	35
Hungarian	404,306	247,018	57	38	38
Slovak	247,555	210,903	32	27	25
Swedish	224,287	136,720	47	20	12
Greek	96,900	138,059	30	19	17
French	183,657	129,894	43	22	18
Ukrainian	60,200	108,376	14	39	39
Croatian	107,094	103,022	12	8	9
Chinese	112,874	95,926	12	14	13
Capatho-Russian	98,500	93,051	12	11	10
Slovene	128,684	92,350	12	10	10
Russian	121,016	64,359	19	43	40
Norwegian	140,705	57,709	37	17	12

Carpatho-Russian refers to the Russian which has a strong admixture of Polish and Hungarian words, with marked differences in pronunciation, too. Most of its publications are purely fraternal and religious, strongly Russian Orthodox, a few including some general news.

Religious and fraternal publications for Norwegian Americans in English, however, are up to 81,000 circulation for a weekly, 34,000 for a monthly, 20,000 for a quarterly and 14,000 for a bi-weekly.

All Swedish newspapers up to 1866 were connected with a church. An effort in 1851 to publish one without religious connections failed within a year in New York City.

Of the periodicals that dropped out of the Swedish-language list this year, three simply switched over to English. This has been the trend in the Scandinavian press; its readers turn naturally to English. They have a big Swedish-language weekly in Chicago, The Svenska Amerikanaren Tribunen (Swedish American Tribune), started in 1876, with 27,100 circulation, nonetheless showing a drop of nearly 2,000 in a year.

Other Swedish-language weeklies are Svea, of Worcester, Mass., 1897, 31,000 circulation, Nordstjernan (Swedish North Star), New York City, 1872, 8,000; Norden (The North), Brooklyn, 1896, 2,300; Svenska Posten (Swedish Post), Seattle, 1886, 3,300, and several other old ones with two or three thousand circulation. Swedish Americans have a half dozen weeklies in English, practically all religious. The Lutherans have 95,000 circulation for a Rock Island, Ill., paper, the Baptists 25,000 for a Chicago one, and the Evangelical Free Church of America 13,000 for one at Minneapolis, which becomes bi-weekly during summer.

The table shows an over-all circulation drop for all nationality groups except the Spanish, Greek and Ukrainian. The comparatively small rise in the Spanish, 65,000 in nearly two decades in spite of the great Puerto Rican influx, shows that the Spanish-speaking American goes into English much more so than the editors of Spanish-language papers care to admit.

The influx of refugees from World War II were enough to be of real benefit to the Ukrainian and Greek minority papers. They have been helped, too, by the stress these communities put on teaching the ancestral tongue in school. One of the most modern school buildings in New York City's Lower East Side, in the shadow of Cooper Union, is the Ukrainian.

Although the Czech press generally has suffered a marked circulation drop, its bilingual Denni Hlasatel (Daily Herald), of Chicago, founded in 1891, has 60,241 daily and Sunday circulation, while Hlasatel (Herald), a Chicago semi-weekly that goes back to 1892, has 61,045. The New Yorkshe Listy (New York News), a tri-weekly launched in 1874, has 12,250, and the Leader-Svoboda-News, a bilingual weekly of El Campo, Tex., 1885, has 6,000. The Czech press is particularly strong in fraternal periodicals. One such is the bilingual weekly Vestnik (Herald), put out by the Slavonic Benevolent Order of Texas, at West, Tex., which reports 33,000 circulation.

The Greek Americans have two New York dailies. The Atlantis, begun in 1894, is a determined supporter of the Greek monarchy, and leans toward the Republican Party in American politics. The National Herald is a little more popular in its appeal, less warm about royalty, and leans toward the Democrats. The former has 19,000 and the latter 17,000 circulation. Atlantis also puts out a bilingual, illustrated monthly news-magazine of the same name, with 13,000 circulation.

Bilingual weeklies are put out in Boston, Kypia-katika Nea (Greek Sunday News), founded 1950, 3,800 circulation; in San Francisco, the New California, 1907, 3,200; in Chicago, Ellenikos-Aster (Greek Star), 1904, 4,200, and in Greek alone in Chicago, the Ellen-ikos Typos (Greek Press), 1912, 3,500, and two in Detroit, the Athenai (Detroit Athens), 1928, 5,300, and the National Greek Tribune, 1922. Significantly, the Hellenic Chronicle, of Boston, a Greek weekly in English, has nearly 18,500 circulation.

Chapter Six

The Jewish-Language Press

Editors speak frankly of the decline of the Jewish-language press almost as a measure of its success. Its disappearance in the measurable future is accepted almost as a matter of faith. Yet it has had the most creative experience of all.

The language is also known as Yiddish, but the newspapers themselves use the word Jewish in English. Yiddish is a corruption of Judische—Jewish in German. The language, as it evolved in the Germanic lands of the Middle Ages, was vastly different than today, and underwent still more changes elsewhere, as in Galicia and Lithuania.

A press also exists in Hebrew, the classical, official language of Israel, which like Arabic is a Semitic tongue, as kind to the ear as Mandarin Chinese, or the Queen's English—distinctly not the Oxford or Brooklyn mispronunciation.

The United States has no Hebrew newspapers. Only Hadoar (The Post), founded in 1921 as a political weekly and bi-weekly by Histadruth Ivrith of America, is in Hebrew, and has 10,000 circulation. The rest are cultural and religious publications.

New York City has three Jewish-language daily papers and Philadelphia one, with a combined circulation of at most 125,000, a drop of more than 25,000 in a year. In 1920 there were four, with 360,-

000 circulation, almost two-thirds more than the 1960 figures.

The Jewish press has sought integration into the life of its community as well as into American life generally practically since its start. Its editors gave themselves the task of teaching their readers how to adjust to the American environment by interpreting the American scene. They themselves had to learn this. In the process, readers and editors together became part of this bright New World, with its heroic grant of status and dignity to the individual, qualities which the Jew had not been granted through most of history, and for which he developed his most intense craving.

Simultaneously, a new Jewish language was molded out of the old, off-beat patois. In this way, the American Jewish press became the crystallizing element and medium for the development of a Jewish literature, which has now spread worldwide, with translations into numerous languages.

This began when, for the first time, politics was explained in the Jewish spoken language. Words and expressions had to be devised. The same problem was met when it came to technology.

The result, during this hey-dey of the Jewish-language press, was eager acceptance of the American melting pot that made for self-expression and prosperity.

The original Jewish press was small and conservative, for Jewish immigration was then only a trickle. The first paper was the Judische Post, begun as a weekly in 1872. The trickle became a flood overnight, and papers sprouted like mushrooms in the Russian woods. A Jewish Gazette, established only two years later, bought out and consolidated twenty Jewish weeklies and dailies.

By 1918, there had been 150 Jewish publications. The papers able to survive were only those that focussed on the interests and needs of the Jewish workingman. Socialism then appeared almost as a matter of faith, and constituted the appeal. The Forwerts (Jewish Daily Forward), which still leads the field, was started in 1897. Its enterprise killed off the remaining Jewish conservative press. Yet the growth of the Jewish-language press, and its cultural success, were achieved through the private enterprise system entirely. This contradiction became more and more recognized, until with the example that Hitler and Stalin gave of the truly vicious monoply into which dogmatic socialism inevitably led, these papers modified their interpretation of socialism, away from economic rigidity toward social reform within a private enterprise framework.

The present-day 65,000 daily and Sunday circulation of the Forward, while big, is a far cry from its 143,716 in 1920, and a considerable drop from its 85,000 reported only the previous year. The other Jewish daily of influence is Der Tog-Morgen Journal (The Day-Jewish Journal), founded in 1914, which began 1960 with a daily and Sunday circulation of 51,000, with 42,000 on Saturday. The year before it reported 64,000 daily and 54,000 on Saturday. The Philadelphia edition of this paper, the only Jewish-language daily printed outside of New York City, reports 3,000 circulation.

The only other daily paper is Morgen Freiheit (Morning Freedom), the communist organ begun in 1922, that claims 8,000, a drop in circulation of about 1,000 for the year.

The New Leader, an anti-totalitarian, English-language weekly magazine of social reform, as contrasted with the old-time, dogmatic socialism that characterized its forebears, recently referred to the Forward in an editorial reminiscing over the history of the Jewish labor movement.

"To name but a few of its components," it said, "the International Ladies Garment Workers' Union, the Capmakers Union, the Jewish Daily Forward, the Workmen's Circle and its network of schools—provides just a hint of the vitality of that movement. For a period of some decades, it performed a double role: it represented an entire way of life for hundreds of thousands of immigrants, and it served as their chief instrument of Americanization, enabling them to channel their vigor and creative spirit into the larger community."

The Jewish press was able to amass a big circulation fast because it could tap the largest immigrant community anywhere. About 1,500,000 Jews, a fourth of the city's population, lived in New York City in 1917. Jewish was the mother tongue of two-thirds of them. More than half a million copies of Jewish papers were sold daily. Only the German-language press was larger, but its distribution was nationwide. Jewish newspapers were sold elsewhere almost only in Boston and Philadelphia.

The Day began in Philadelphia in 1900, and still survives in combined form. The only Jewish weekly newspaper, the Wisconsin Jewish Chronicle, was begun in 1921 in Milwaukee. A bi-weekly, the Freie Arbeiter Stimme (Free Voice of Labor), was started in 1890 as an anarchist paper to compete with a Socialist paper, the Arbeiter Zeitung, founded the same year by the United Hebrew Trades. Students of the Jewish language say that its development can be traced by the changes made in the style of writing in the Arbeiter Zeitung. This anarchist sheet attracted readers who had not the slightest interest in its political creed by the high literary tone of its writing. Its first editor became well known for a column in which he criticized rejected manuscripts for the benefit of writers generally, laying aside his political armor for a cultural garb.

Jewish-language editors had an unparalleled opportunity to produce a balanced, interesting newspaper because they were in a position to diversify its contents in a way most foreign-language editors could not. Immigrants of other nationalities were mainly of one type, belonging to an identical work category and outlook. One class, the peasantry usually, would leave a homeland area. This limited the subject matter upon which these other editors could draw to attract readers. Many if not most of the immigrants in those communities came to America intending to raise a quick fortune and then return to Europe. What they found was so attractive they usually stayed, or their minds were changed for them by international developments. The outbreak of World War I made return unthinkable. Then the second generation, when it became old enough to express itself, would not hear of leaving the United States.

But the Jewish immigrants came intending to stay. They emigrated to the United States as a composite group. All the inhabitants of a village, from workers to shopkeepers to teachers, would pull up stakes and leave Europe with good riddance.

The outstanding editor in the Jewish-language press was The Forward's Abraham Cahan. He had been a successful English-language journalist and special writer for the old N. Y. Sun and the old N. Y. Evening Post, which insisted on a high standard in writing, and he also contributed to leading national magazines. The board of managers of The Forward appealed to him to bring his experience to it, in order to keep it alive, for the paper had a bare 4,000 circulation and was deeply in debt. Cahan at once agreed. The first thing he did was to take the lofty tone out of the writing and bring the subject matter down to earth, discarding theoretical discussion. He brought over the technique he had learned on the English-language press. He made the written language the same as the spoken, a revolutionary departure. He replaced articles on economic materialism with feature stories about pavement romances and bazaar life. Circulation tripled in two months; in a few years it was well over a hundred thousand. Profits replaced debts.

Adolph Held, now an International Ladies Garment Workers Union official, was city editor of The Forward when World War I broke out. He remembers Cahan walking into the newsroom one day soon after, glancing at several war dispatches and then asking the copy reader: "What's this about kilometers? Does your mother know what a kilometer is?" The copy editor admitted she didn't. "Then what's the point in running it?" he asked. He took a pile of war dispatches out of the incoming basket. "We'll not use any more of these war telegrams," he announced. The staff was stunned. "I'll write a two-column article each day, putting all these facts together and explaining them so your mother now will be able to understand," he announced. Within a month circulation rose by 20,000.

In a sense Cahan edited the whole Jewish-language press in America. All the other papers watched The Forward in his day and were careful to pick up the innovations he instituted in modernizing the language and making news meaningful to his readers.

The immigrant press, which appeared in the Jewish and Italian languages principally in New York, as well as the German and to a lesser extent, in other European tongues, had to meet the competition of the English-language papers, and this presented an impossible task. A scramble developed among English-language papers for readers from the foreign-language field. The Jewish-language press probably took the biggest loss, for it was the most vulnerable.

One New York paper has lately come to represent a new, overt stage in this competition for the Jewish reader, in which the circulation pitch is aimed at him specifically, so much so that others in the Jewish-language press referred to it as their main competition at present. This paper makes its appeal to all specific minorities, putting a strident stress on issues which might gain readers also from among the Puerto Ricans, Negroes, Italians and other minority groups. The drum is beaten for each as a separate group with its own grievances, rather than as part of an American society with positive, common problems. Its articles portray the police as the villain, and the rapist or killer appears to be the one to receive the sympathy as a frustrated individual, rather than the victim, who tends to be shunted aside. This is a new circulation twist, extremely productive circulation-wise, but the effect it has on national unity in a crowded community of different racial and national groups is another matter.

The tabloids were the most successful in gaining readers from the foreign-language papers. They also made a pitch for the Negro minority. An executive for the Amsterdam News, the big Negro weekly in Manhattan, that claims a 45,000 circulation, told me that the N. Y. Post and The Mirror, rather than the Negro press, constituted his main, direct competition.

The Mirror, a morning paper in the Hearst chain that comes out early the previous evening, gives over-all coverage to what is of most sensational interest to all persons indiscriminately, while providing, for instance, the sort of statistics which members of these different groups use as a basis for the numbers game so prevalent in Harlem.

The N. Y. Daily News, which has the biggest circulation in America, has been notably successful in attracting readers from all minority elements, providing them with a least common denominator of news and opinion. Significantly, it follows the staid, old newspaper technique of making a uniformly balanced appeal to all, whether Slav minority or Puritan descendant.

Chapter Seven

The Slavic Press

1. THE INDOMITABLE POLES

So long as a Pole remains alive in the United States, and can scrounge a few sheets of paper and some old type, Free Poland will not die. So long as Poland remains unfree, there will be plenty of American Poles living in an ambivalent state, fighting the ages-old Polish fight, yet so well blended into the American type that they can hardly be distinguished from those with English forebears.

One might, on the basis of the record, go even farther. So long as the Polish and other Slavic papers exist in the United States, with Ukrainian, Lithuanian and the Czech as examples, the foreign-language press will keep reminding old American families that liberty has to be guarded by eternal vigilance and a readiness to fight and die for it. These Eastern Europeans recognize, from sad experience, the stages that mark the loss of freedom, and know full well how accommodating men can let it slip through their fingers. They know the tactics, from having seen them used against themselves. I have frequently heard these new Americans exclaim in horror over the inclination in old American circles, made comfortable by push-buttons and gadgets, to take liberty for granted, like the air we breathe.

Perhaps this ringing of the alarm bell when they see fire may be their most important repayment to the America that gave them haven. What greater repayment could they make?

The Polish-language press, and that of all these naturalized citizens who have seen their native lands despoiled, cry out against the "co-existence" lullaby. They remember the words and music from having heard it sung to them.

Their warnings would be even more specific if their editors had not been given so-called friendly admonitions by "official sources" to speak and tread softly, and sometimes not to speak at all. This is nothing new. The truth about the Katyn Massacre was kept from the American public for years when these foreign-language editors knew exactly who had perpetrated the genocide and how. This was disclosed to the American public only years later by a select Senate Committee. If the truth which these foreign-language editors, and also some foreign-language broadcasters, were trying to bring out had not been silenced, the rules which were then being set up for the United Nations at San Francisco would have been very different, without the crippling provisions that have handicapped it ever since. This came out at the hearings, too.

A former Hearst correspondent, Alan Cranston, later with the Office of War Information, admitted having exercised such pressure. Casimir Soron of Buffalo, a Detroit newspaperman, who had been working in the foreign language press field for eight years, told of being put off the air for telling about Soviet Russia's involvement in the Katyn Massacre.

The hearings also heard how the largest Polish-language paper in the United States, along with other Slavic papers, warned that Allied wartime policy was directly leading to the self-defeating, dead end street of Soviet Russian conquest of Eastern Europe. This was hushed up by the easy device of being branded pro-Nazi propaganda. Alvin E. O'Konski, Congressman from Wisconsin, remarked: "This is actually what happened, did it not?"

The fighting Polish-language press is ahead of most in number. Its seven dailies, four of which are bilingual, are exceeded only by the Spanish and Chinese. Its 21 weeklies, nine bilingual, are 12 behind the German, but are up in the lead along with the Italian, Hungarian and Spanish papers.

The Polish dailies range between 21,000 and 35,000 in circulation. These figures are even more impressive when realized that foreign-language papers are frequently fraternal organs as well, and that an average copy has more persons reading it than its English counterpart. They are not discarded in buses and subways. An ordinary American will buy several papers to read; not so in the foreign-language field, where one paper is bought and read by a number of persons.

The Polish weeklies include Gwiazda Polarna (Polish Star), Stevens Point, Wisc., bilingual, started in 1892, with 17,100 circulation; Przewodnik Katolicki (Catholic Leader), New Britain, Conn., 1907, 21,000; Ameryka Echo (American Echo), Toledo, Ohio, 1886, 17,000; Czas (Times), Brooklyn, 1905, 13,500; Straz (The Guard), Scranton, Pa., 1897, 9,500; Slowo Pol-

skie (Polish Word), Utica, N. Y., 1909, 7,300, and
Gwiazda (Polish Star), Philadelphia, bilingual, 1902,
8,100.

The Polish National Alliance of the United States
owns the bilingual Dziennik Zwiazkowy (Polish Daily
Unity), of Chicago, begun in 1918, whose 35,000 circulation makes it the largest Polish daily. It follows
an independent policy on American politics. While
showing frequent sympathy for the Eisenhower administration, for instance, it did not budge from its
insistence on full Polish freedom. Dziennik Zwiazkowy
never softened toward the Warsaw communist regime,
seeing in its concessions only a ruse. The Alliance
also publishes a fraternal organ, the bi-weekly Zgoda
(Unity). Its 1881 start makes it the oldest Polish
publication in America. Ayer's Directory credits
Zgoda with 140,000 circulation, but the Alliance says
all its 350,000 members see it.

Another big, bilingual Polish daily in Chicago,
Dziennik Chicagoski (Polish Daily News), founded
in 1890, has 21,000 circulation. The Resurrectionist
Fathers publish it, and its attitude toward the Polish
regime is middle-of-the-road, avoiding sharp criticism
of the Gomulka regime, while striving toward full
Polish independence. In American politics it is independent on the side of the Democrats.

The sports page of several Polish-language dailies
is in English, to attract the younger element. Articles
of special interest to the new generation also are often
published in English on a special page. Significantly,
few foreign dispatches are put on this page, which
focusses on local personalities and local happenings.

An interpretative summary of some foreign development is given instead.

An English page with its own editor is printed by Dziennik Polski (Polish Daily News), of Detroit, which boasts: "56 Years of Service to Americans of Polish Descent—1904-1960." Its nearly 35,000 circulation, while big, is a drop for it. Its publisher was a Polish Republican leader in Michigan, Frank Januszewski, who was succeeded at his death by his wife, Stefania. The paper has since relaxed its former staunch Republican stand. In international affairs, it is against the Warsaw regime.

Immigrants of all nationalities are baffled by American comic strips, and frequently have little patience with them. Their sense of humor is different, and they lack the background in America. The rapid transformation that has been achieved in one generation is graphically shown by the three comics on the English page of Dziennik Polski.

Another daily which follows an independent policy, opposed to the Warsaw regime, is Kuryer Codzienny (Polish Daily Courier), of South Boston, founded in 1913, which has 30,000 circulation. A similar voice is raised by the daily Wiadomosci Codzienne (Polish Daily News), of Cleveland, started in 1915, which has 28,000 circulation.

The oldest Polish daily is Kuryer Polski (Polish Courier), of Milwaukee, that was launched in 1888, and has 20,000 circulation. Although traditionally considered Republican, it was leaning toward the Democrats in 1959. On Poland, while anti-communist, observers say it is holding back its punch.

The weekly Gwiazda Polarna (Polar Star) in Wisconsin, gained a certain attention when it was the only one of the Polish-language newspapers, except the outright communist organ, not to criticize Khrushchev during his 1959 tour of the United States. This paper follows a pro-Warsaw line, urging that "realities" be faced. Its editor, Adam Bartosz, was a welcome visitor to Warsaw, and the paper is recognized as a softening-up influence generally. The same publishers put out another weekly, Rolnik (The Farmer), that began in 1892 and has only 700 circulation. Geared to the farmer, it assumes much the same attitude, although running less such material.

The communist paper, put out at Detroit, is the weekly, bilingual Glos Ludowy (People's Voice), going back to 1909, which has 3,000 circulation.

A hard-hitting, highly professional daily in New York City is Nowy Swiat (Morning World), that started in 1919, and has nearly 25,000 circulation. Nowy Swiat adopted a formula for economic survival which permits it to fearlessly raise its voice in the independent, American manner. When its publisher died, those who produced the paper took over ownership by buying stock in it. At the same time, they gave over certain pages to the Sons of Poland and to the Polish Union in the United States, thus making Nowy Swiat their official organ.

These pages are made up to look like miniature newspapers. One, entitled "Urja Polska" (Polish Unity), generally runs several English-language columns. The 18,000 membership of the Sons of Poland and the 28,000 in the Polish Union were thus brought into intimate relationship with Nowy Swiat.

Ignace Morawski, the Nowy Swiat editor and general manager, is an outstanding example in the foreign-language field of a journalist of the highest cultural background and the finest professional standing. Soon after he arrived in the United States more than fifty years ago, he started out as a cub reporter on the old N. Y. Tribune. He has shown his versatility with languages the hard way, by working on Russian, German, French and Ukrainian papers in America, thereby gaining a probably unparalleled, broader all-around newspaper experience than possibly any other newspaperman.

In World War I, he served on the Foreign Language Committee set up by George Creel. His voice is well known in Poland, for he has broadcast his freedom messages for years. Although more than 70 years of age, he presents a virile figure, tall and lithe. He is precisely the Polish type—although utterly American for a generation—that both Hitler and Stalin rounded up for extermination in their collective genocide program during World War II, knowing that their totalitarian regimes could not endure if he and those of his kind were able to survive. Unlike Winston Churchill, he has not waited to retire before conducting a one-man show of his oils and charcoal sketches. His English-speaking editorial column appears daily on the first page of Nowy Swiat. He packs it with exclusive information. This would be a fulltime task for a normal worker, but he recently took charge of the business department, too, while continuing editorial supervision of the paper.

News of deep concern to the United States on what is happening behind the fluttering curtain of official

communiques in a country such as Poland finds its way
with extraordinary frequency into the pages of Nowy
Swiat, and papers like it in a number of foreign languages. This is understandable because of the special
relationship that certain of their editors and reporters
have developed over the years in those countries. The
intimate contact they built up through devious channels is the equivalent of an intelligence service, yet one
of great reliance because of the very personal relationship between all contacts down the line. They had to
do this, for their readers would not put up with being
given only what appears in the English-language
press. An attitude I grew familiar with in meeting
these foreign-language editors was the resigned des-
peration with which they would refer to important
events and developments first reported in detail and
explained in their paper, but ignored until it was too
late to do anything about them.

The record of accuracy on vital information on
foreign affairs achieved by courageous foreign-
language papers is evidence that we have here an invaluable source of information for the discriminating
analyst in the editorial offices of English-language
publications and in government bureaus. Time and
again, the information sought and often not found by
our government attaches abroad has already appeared
on the pages of our foreign-language papers. Foreign-
language editors frequently reach a different conclusion on foreign news than others, based on their
greater knowledge in depth.

2. IN THE RUSSIAN CHARACTER

The Russian-language press in general, contrary to popular impression, is small in number and circulation. While interest in it has expanded tremendously outside of the Russian-language community, it has fallen off a half in over-all circulation, from an estimated 121,016 in 1942 to 64,359 in 1959.

The high professional quality and courageous editorial outlook of one Russian-language newspaper, the Novoye Russkoye Slovo (New Russian Word), accounts for its daily and Sunday circulation of 23,250, an increase of nearly a thousand over the past year at a time when the tendency in practically the whole foreign-language newspaper field is almost all the other way. Present-day Russian immigrants, all escapees, are much too few to much influence circulation. Second and third generation Russians take to America like a duck to water. They usually read only the English-language press. Many who would have immersed themselves completely in American society, without a glance toward Europe, retain their interest out of a sense of responsibility toward their stricken forebears.

Indeed, this is the main stimulant to the foreign-language press nowadays, stemming what otherwise would be a precipitous drop in circulations all around.

The daily Rossiya (Russia)—it observes a two-day weekend and a week off in summer—has a circulation below 2,500. This figure seems to be declining with the death rate among old White Russian emigres, who differ strikingly from the World War II Russian exodus. The former still speak of the Czar in reverential tones, and some even consider the restoration of the monarchy possible. The knightly emblems alongside the paper's masthead sets its tone, quaint as a flimsy, antique chair.

Except for this fantasy, Rossiya, that was started in 1933, could have picked up circulation from among the World War II refugees from the Soviet Union. As a group, they are unalterably anti-communist. People raised under communism are usually more inflexibly opposed to it than those who have never experienced it. These post-World War II expatriates can no more take a monarchial appeal seriously than an American would consider enthroning Queen Elizabeth in the White House.

Five Russian papers appear as dailies, two in San Francisco and three in New York City, including the communist organ, Russky Golos, that claims 1916 as its date of origin, and nearly 6,000 as its circulation. In addition, a weekly, Nashe Vremya (Modern Time), founded in 1050, also at the Golden Gate, has about 1,500 circulation. The daily Russkaya Zhizn (Russian Life), begun at the same city in 1925, which takes Sunday and Monday off, is much the local paper, catering to the social and cultural life of the large, Russian-speaking community in California.

The Russian colony in San Francisco, as reflected by this paper, live a more provincial existence of the old type than those in Greater New York. Russkaya Zhizn is a smalltown paper and looks it—its page is the enormous size produced by our most primitive printing presses. The Russian community on the Pacific coast is more closely knit than that of New York.

The remaining Rusian daily, Novaya Zaria (New Dawn), of San Francisco, begun in 1928, has never recovered from a period of intimacy with the Soviet Consulate. The paper shows no policy of its own, lacking editorials, and with few outside contributors.

Novoye Slovo, the oldest daily, going back to 1910 —it celebated its 60th anniversary in 1960— has a greater circulation than all the others together. Indeed, it has more than a third of the total circulation of all Russian periodicals, of whatever nature.

Novo Slovo's emphasis differs strikingly from that of the other Russian publications. They represent generally one or another group outlook which, no matter how deeply felt, is nonetheless only a small part of the whole.

Although overall circulation took a big dive, the number of Russian-language publications rose from 19 in 1942 to 40 in 1960. Quarterlies, monthlies and bi-monthlies are put out by every sort of nostalgic organization, from the Association of Russian Imperial Naval Officers in America, Inc. and the Gallipoli Society in the U. S. A. to the Union of Russian Jurists Abroad, and what is simply called Group of Kuban Officers in the U. S.

These are not splinter groups. They are the gathering places of people who have been in the United States for a long time now, and who in a great number of cases have blended into the American setting. They sentimentally retain this small group attachment as their only reminder of the past. They read the English-language papers, although many also subscribe to Novoye Slovo, and to a lesser extent to Rossiya or some Russian paper on the West Coast.

Others do fit into the splinter group description, having isolated themselves from American influences, living in the distant past, and feeding on the particular periodical which best brings back old memories.

Novoye Slovo is as full of the present as the others are of yesteryear. Although in Russian, it puts its prime emphasis on American news, on what is happening in the United States and locally in New York and other metropolitan areas where people of Russian background congregate. It is outspokenly American rather than just pro-American; it has consistently presented and explained the American way of life, its duties and privileges. At the same time, it scrupulously keeps up with foreign news, especially Soviet Russian developments.

This seems to make it more consistent in its unabashed analysis of Soviet Russian news than some of the others in the Russian-language field. The latter at times appear influenced in their judgment by a consciousness that they are Russian, their nationalist nostalgia softening their point of view with the years. The communists benefit from this sentimental attitude. Although this trait is noticeable in the post-World War I emigration, it is not discernible among post-World War II escapees and their publications.

The latter, instead of being classified as White Russians, may be better identified as anti-communist Soviet Russians, for they were raised in Soviet Russia. But like the Hungarian youth of the freedom uprising, and the young Chinese communist troops who refused to return to Red China after their capture in the Korean war, hatred of communism has permeated the marrow of their bones. They were raised on it!

A big fraction of this post-World War I Russian emigration, perhaps most of it, felt as bitterly toward the original Kerensky regime, which aimed at a democratic government similar to America's, as it did toward Lenin's, which was able to capture the moderate revolution through the connivance of an almost unbelievably nearsighted Junker element in the German imperial army, that had become desperate over approaching defeat. How the German people, and the world, have paid for this blindly clever piece of early psychological warfare!

The Russian emigration all along has been a persecuted exodus, first by the Czar, mainly of Jews, and then by the communists, of so-called "class enemies." The former period went on during the 1870s through the 1920s. The latter period has lasted from then on. This, too, may be divided into two broad divisions, the White Russians and the anti-communist Soviet Russians. The former are mainly the nobility and the upper merchant element, the latter the remainder of these, and step by step, down the ladder to include other merchants and businessmen generally, the upper, middle and finally the lower middle class, farmers who were not hired hands or not poor, and ultimately, workers and peasants who demonstrated capacity for independent thought.

Mark Weinbaum, as editor of Novoye Slovo, estimates that only 30 per cent of his readers have a good or better knowledge of English. The meaningful, pertinent articles he runs enables these others especially to keep up with domestic and foreign affairs. The paper estimates that 80 per cent of its readers have become American citizens, and is justifiably proud of its part in this Americanization process.

Novoye Slovo has followed a policy of bringing the controversial out into the open for airing and settlement. Thus it was with the Americanization issue. Nothing could have been more controversial. Was it honorable to renounce allegiance to one's motherland at any time, for any reason? This was an agonizing and fiercely debated issue among the White Russians. A statement by Mr. Weinbaum on April 22, 1945, printed in the concert program for the newspaper's thirty-fifth anniversary celebration, summarizes these growing pains. He wrote:

"The Russkoye Slovo, as it was called at first, was started by immigrants and for immigrants. Its early editors had little knowledge of the English tongue and still less of American institutions. When one of them read that during an election of a speaker of the House there were six scattering votes, he wrote, 'Mr. Scattering received six votes.' Another editorial writer ful minated against the then President for not abolishing 'Wall Street' by ukase.

"In Russia these men fought the Czar. Here 'Wall Street' became their enemy. And beyond 'Wall Street' they saw little in American life that was worth preserving.

"About two decades ago readers of the Novoye Russkoye Slovo were hotly debating in its columns the value of American citizenship. Many held the view that it was dishonorable to renounce allegiance to the mother country for the sake of American citizenship. By that time we in the Novoye Russkoye Slovo did not subscribe to such opinions. We combatted them carefully but persistently and with very gratifying results.

"Because many Russians did not like to tell that they had become American citizens, we made it a point favorably to mention such facts in our columns. It took hold and later we were asked to do so by the new citizens themselves. Once we were pleased and amused when a Russian octogenarian proudly presented to us his card on which under his name he had the following line: 'Russian General—American Citizen.'

"Today many of those who twenty years ago argued against becoming American citizens are intensely proud of their citizenship. They have given their sons and daughters to the armed forces of the Republic and are otherwise supporting our war effort.

"We take pride in this. And with all modesty we must say that we have a share in it and even if we had done nothing else, the Novoye Russkoye Slovo has justified its existence. In the course of years it became an American newspaper in purpose, outlook and ideals."

Continuing in a different vein, he added:

"We are proud because one of our early editors was Leo Pasvolsky, now special assistant to the Secretary of State, and that among our present contributing editors we count such men as Ivan Bunin, the Nobel Prize winner, Mark Aldanov, the noted author, and many other well-known writers and journalists."

Dramatic scenes, frequently simple in their pathos, sometimes historic, occur in the editor's sanctum. Its door is always open, as it used to be with all newspaper editors. Mr. Weinbaum saw a lady standing there one day, nervous and shaking. She grasped hold of

the door. "Should I close it?" she asked, and before
he could reply she had shut it. Patiently he opened it.
"There is no need for fear here," he told her. The
lady was Mrs. Oksana Stepanova Kasenkina, the
Soviet Russian schoolteacher who was seeking to stay
in America and not go back to the Soviet Union. This
was a major lesson in what America meant; indeed, it
was her sensing of this that led her to take the step
that nearly cost her life when she leaped out of the
window of the Soviet Consulate General.

During the past generation, an editor's initial task
was to teach immigrants what a newspaper was; they
had no conception. News, editorials and advertising
were all one to them. Frequently they sent money to
the paper to buy a watch or something else being advertised. Sometimes they came and asked to see the
merchandise, and could not understand why it was
not on display. They thought a newspaper was some
new-fangled American store, and that everything advertised belonged to the newspaper and was on sale
on its premises. Some thought it was a kind of bank.
The role of a newspaper in a democracy was one of the
most difficult problems for them to grasp. The
foreign-language papers had to begin at the bottom
to teach how democracy worked out in practice.

When Mr. Weinbaum came to America in December
of 1913, there were two Russian papers, neither a
daily. One was the present Russkoye Slovo, then appearing three times a week, and the other Novy Mir
(New World). The latter was a socialist publication
until the Bolsheviks took it over and made Bukharin
and then Trotsky editor. It began in 1910 as non-

partisan and progressive, becoming a daily and prosperous under the impetus of World War 1.

Mr. Weinbaum wrote for such newspapers as the old N. Y. American and The Tribune before going into Russian-language journalism. In order to be able to do this, he arranged for a special college course that consisted entirely of subjects dealing with the English language. He had been raised in the Ukraine, then known as Little Russia, not far from the old Austro-Hungarian border.

The outstanding columnist of the foreign-language press, one of the greatest in America, is also on Novoye Slovo. He signs himself "Argus." He's a bright-faced, robust little figure full of vigor, whose real name is known to few; it's Macy Eisenstadt. No more devastating writing appears anywhere, with an earthly humor that belongs to the era of Ring Lardner and George Ade, when Americans weren't afraid of belly laughter. He's an old-timer on the staff.

He started his column, already signing it "Argus", when he was a youthful newspaperman in Riga before the Russian Revolution. An indication of his style can be gleaned from the following aphorisms, dealing with communism, from some of his columns:

"In the upside-down language of the communists, black is white, white is red, and red is progressive."

"The same people who insist that the communists are the most honest people on earth also insist that ex-communists are the biggest liars."

"An American who thinks that the Soviet Union is the most wonderful country in the world is called by Moscow an 'American patriot'. But an American who thinks that America is the most wonderful country in the world is called by Moscow an 'imperialist'."

"We understand that the Soviet Ambassador will be recalled to Moscow shortly. Three bottles of Coca Cola were found hidden in his office."

As evidence that he can employ the same keen wit on the domestic scene, of a sort reminiscent of Will Rogers is the following:

"I sometimes wonder if Helen Keller would have been so perseverant in overcoming her handicaps if she had started in our age of communist propaganda and TV commercials."

A large segment of the Slavic press, from the Estonian to the Ukrainian, translates from the Novoye Slovo, and frequently follows its editorial lead.

Since the appearance of the Sputnik, subscriptions for the paper by colleges and universities have markedly risen, for use in language study and to obtain Russian background. The paper also circulates abroad, and a batch of copies is known to be sent regularly to Moscow.

Again and again in the foreign-language press, the results show that the editor who makes his paper first of all an American newspaper with emphasis on news about the "old country", who courageously fights subversion here and communism abroad, wins the trust of his readers.

Chapter Eight

Others Very Present

1. HUNGARY'S TORTURED VOICE

Hungarians have long, unforgiving memories. Hungary has passed through more diverse schisms, bloody factional fights and wars within the memory of many still alive than probably any other European people. Heated memories are kept on fire by knowledge that the struggle still goes on with no sign of surcease.

The Hungarian-language press in America reflects every bit of these bitternesses and hates. Here alone is there opportunity for their unrestricted outlet. As a consequence, there is no peace between the innumerable factions—and factions within factions— that the various publications represent.

Other minority groups suffer from the same crippling ailment, but possibly none so acutely. Part of this discord has the earmarks of being artificially engendered, as a wedge-driving or other psychological warfare tactic, to prevent an effective anti-communist front from forming.

The Hungarian-language press has been plagued by conspiracy from its earliest years. A sordid page was the brazen plot of the Austro-Hungarian government, even before World War I, to control the Hungarian immigrants in the United States, along with those of other racial and nationality groups in the empire. The primary tactic was to keep each at the throats of all the others. This vulnerability still remains, and still is being exploited. A branch of the Hungarian Postal Savings Bank was secretly set up in America under the cover name of Transatlantic Trust Co. The bank failed to subvert any appreciable number of immigrants, but it did channel a great part of their hard-earned savings into Hungary. The Hungarian clergy in the United States were paid a salary by the Austro-Hungarian government, exactly as at home. Their churches were used in barefaced attempts to block the Americanization process. Prayer books branded as traitors those who sent their children to American schools.

The bank, taking advantage of the Hungarian-language press struggle for survival, captured most newspapers by manipulated advertising. A bank executive reported to his government in Budapest that in a short time, "the American-Magyar press entirely" would be in the control of his agents. The same corruption spread to the Austrian press, as well. World War I Senate hearings exposed this whole sorry mess.

The first successful export of communism, although temporary, was to Hungary in 1918 in the form of Bela Kun's soviet republic. Hungarian aristocracy had been guilty of shocking arrogance and medieval exploitation. Of course, there were many noble persons of all ranks who would have no part in these excesses. They were too few. Initially, this situation was to the Red advantage. But people soon were disillusioned with them so that when the Fascists and the Nazis came along, they had little difficulty in obtaining local recruits. Many were so bitter against communism that they went all the way to the other extreme in combatting them. This, too, had its reaction. More became Communists out of sheer revulsion against the right extremists. The crazy spiral soared up and up. Each extremism, in effect, recruited for the other. This was how France, too, was softened up for its World War II debacle.

All this extremism brought the Hungarian-language press in the United States up against a stark problem. What was to be the reception, for instance, for a refugee from the Bela Kun Red republic, who had worked with it until it fell, but now saw through its wickedness and insisted on taking a leading role in fighting communism? Should those who had seen through the evil from the beginning, who had never compromised themselves, take a back seat? Could they trust these Johnny-come-latelies? How could the sincere be distinguished from the sheer opportunist or from the Communist provocateur, of which there were many? As for the later refugees themselves, they were frankly skeptical about the qualities and character of those who had not, like they, stayed home and gone through the mill.

This mutual suspicion, aggravated perhaps by traits inherited from the Nomadic and Turkic past, coagulated into blind hatred, susceptible to no reasoning. The fiercest charges and counter-charges are hurled between those who alike claim to be fighting the communists the most, each insisting that it alone can be trusted with the responsibility.

Unfortunately, as is generally true, when attention is riveted upon the negative, enough of it is found to justify any damnation. This is very obviously the case in this sad state of affairs. Nowhere more than in the ranks of the Hungarian-language press can the Biblical injunction be more appropriate: "He that is without sin among you, let him first cast a stone . . . "

The first Soviet Republic in Hungary undeniably had a big segment of Jews in it, and this has remained to plague the present, although communism now recognizes in Jewry an implacable foe. The earliest anti-Reds, those who fought and fled from the Hungary of Bela Kun, cannot forgive these men. As a result, they still wallow in the anti-Semitic morass. The terminology and tone of Goebbels and the middle 1930s still can be found in some Hungarian-language newspaper columns.

Somewhere, clandestine operations of a type called "black" in World War II seem lurking under the surface. The frenetic insistence that no anti-communist can be trusted who had once had any relationship with the Reds, the violent condemnation on the same basis even of those who led the heroic revolt of October, 1956, which would exclude even the youths of the Communist Party school, who fought the Reds the most fiercely, the constant harping on the Jews in the Bela Kun regime, all this fits neatly into a propaganda warfare pattern that benefits only Moscow.

The Hungarian - language press has two long-established dailies with a commendable circulation. The first daily published was Szabadsag (Liberty), of Cleveland, begun in 1891, 22,000 circulation. Amerikai Magyar Nepszava (American-Hungarian People's Voice), founded in 1901 in New York City, has 21,500. Twenty weeklies include one of 19,000 circulation, the

Wisconsini Magyarsag (Wisconsin Hungarians), at
Milwaukee, founded in 1924. Others are: Az Ember
(The Man), of New York City, that claims 13,500
circulation, much of whose advertising space deals
with transactions with the Soviet Bloc; Chicago es
Kornyeke (Chicago and Vicinity), of Chicago,
launched in 1906, 12,500 circulation; the bilingual
Southwest Journal, of Detroit, begun in 1932, 10,500,
and the somewhat atavistic Szabad Magyarsag (Free
Hungarians), a bilingual begun only in 1956, claiming 6,500 circulation.

Hungarian publications of all kinds last year totaled 250,000 circulation, 150,000 less than in 1942.

Part of the Hungarian press reflects the spirit of
what history may well regard as the finest page in
the inglorious chapter of our mid-Twentieth Century.
This, of course, was the successful revolt in Hungary,
crushed by Moscow tanks that came back when Washington surprised the Kremlin by not even recognizing
the brave, new regime. The bitterness created by this
is unconcealed in the Hungarian dailies and in much
of the rest of its press; how deep and deadening this
must be behind the Iron Curtain itself!

A flow of 15,000 refugees then poured into the
United States, slightly slowing up the decline in circulations, comparable in some small way to the flood
that came our way after the Kossuth Revolt in Hungary in 1848, which likewise was crushed by the Russian military fist, then the Czar's. The Hungarian-
language press has marked this parallel, and has noted,
too, that the apparent failure of the 1848 revolt nonetheless tolled the ultimate end of the all-powerful
regime of that day.

The first Hungarian paper in the United States was established by heroes of the 1848 revolt who escaped here through Austria, a weekly called Szamuzottek Lappja, or Newspaper of the Exiles.

The Hungarian press has gone through three stages in America, more or less as other minorities. The first immigrants were almost all peasants. They were unconcerned about politics and came seeking a living. The first to become editors were often eggheads who were aloof from their readers and who readily expressed contempt for what they considered crude American customs.

The Hungarian papers that survived learned to adapt themselves to the needs of their peasant-worker readers, and published enlightening articles, for instance about immigration and naturalization. Even in this roundabout way, the American environment was overpowering. The untutored mind of the simple immigrant was wide open to new influences, and welcomed them. Paid anti-American propaganda and the closed minds of so-called intellectuals whose eyes were glued on Europe had slight influence over them.

The next phase came with Hungary's two-thirds dismemberment at Versailles. Many of those who were displaced and impoverished by it sought to re-establish their lives in the United States. These immigrants were generally the educated, but largely from factory and commerce. They came here bitter over the peace terms. This was what they wanted to read about, and the minority press now began to represent their mood. For the first time it sought to influence American opinion and American governing circles. The hardly concealed objective was to create a situation in

Europe which could make possible the return of these people.

Some of the earlier papers stuck to the old line that they had learned by experience, encouraging their readers to become citizens and avoiding what could be regarded as putting pressure on Washington.

The inherent strength of the American environment proved its mettle once more, for most of those who came with the idea of remaining temporarily ended up by becoming citizens and settling down. They became milder in their attitudes, losing their ardor for European affairs, molding into American society. Some of the most impassioned editors and writers went through this process. Our public schools were often the yeast in this Americanization. Children became thoroughly American, and brought this influence home with them. Some immigrants did go back, of course, but a number of them returned, this time to make it forever.

The years between World Wars I and II can be divided between this revisionist period and a persecution period. The latter ushered in the third period, that continued through World War II and its aftermath. Hitler's madness gave it its impetus, which led to the exodus of Jews, other anti-Nazis, and some not directly threatened, but who saw the hope of the future in America. These new arrivals, too, were mostly the educated, whether shopkeepers or scientists. Many of the latter came, including an Hungarian Nobel Prize winner.

This third stage brought about an American format and outlook in much of the foreign-language press, something that had been developing for years.

2.   THE STOLID FINNS

The Finnish is one of the persevering, long-established communities in America, whose press has seen its readership drift away. The editor of one of the largest remaining Finnish newspapers in a private conversation gave his publication only fifteen more years of life.

The first inroad, as in the foreign-language field generally, was the acceptance of English-language advertisements. Advertising, for all its shortcomings, has been second to none in the Americanizing process on practically all fronts. The next was the inclusion of English-language articles, so as to hold on as long as possible to those already slipping away. If lucky, this editor hoped that his paper would be able to switch over completely into English, but wasn't optimistic about it.

In addition there has been a steady drift from dailies to less frequent publication, hastened by the tendency among Americans of Finnish ancestry to move out of their community into a mixed American one, gradually losing touch with Finnish affairs. An example was the recent Finnish Independence Day, that used to be celebrated in Brooklyn by a big gathering with a great deal of merriment, all the proceedings in Finnish. This time only a small number attended, with few of the youth, and the only words heard in Finnish was its national anthem, sung by a small knot of hardy oldtimers.

Two dailies dropped out last year, leaving only one in Fitchburg, Mass., the Raivaaja (Pioneer), begun in 1905, 4,200 circulation. Industrialisti (Industrialist), of Duluth, Minn., founded in 1917, changed to a tri-weekly, 4,100 circulation. The Red-tinted Tyomies-Eteepain (Workingman-Forward), of Superior, Wisc., begun in 1903, also became a tri-weekly, claiming 3,200 circulation.

Two other tri-weeklies are Amerikan Suometar (American Spirit of Finland), that goes back to 1899, 3,000 circulation, and Minnesotan Uutiset (Minnesota News), of New York Mills, Minn., 1917, 7,100 circulation. One semi-weekly, the New Yorkin Uutiset (Finnish New York News), of Brooklyn, founded 1907, has 3,500 circulation.

Of four Finnish-language weeklies, the largest is Tyovaen Osuustoimintalehti (Cooperative Weekly), begun in 1930, 5,500 circulation. The others are the one in Calumet, Mich., that produced a separate, English-written offspring; Attaja (Helper), of Ironwood, Mich., 1906, 1,900, and Naisten Viiri (Women's Banner), of Superior, Wisc., 1910, 3,200.

Chapter Nine

In Asian Characters

1. THE CHINESE PRESS

Eight daily newspapers are published in Chinese on the American mainland. Although there were ten when 1960 began, this leaves Chinese up in front in dailies, along with the Spanish. Chinese-language papers are said to be read by a greater proportion of the 150,000 persons with Chinese blood in them in the United States than those of any other minority.

An intensive effort is being made to teach Chinese to the new generation by private lessons after school, but this is only moderately successful, because of the extreme intricacy of Chinese writing, and the phenomenal demand it makes on memory. Every word is represented by a symbol like the dollar sign in English. The entire written language—its caligraphy—has no alphabet or phonetics, but is made up of such "characters," which depend wholly on memory.

American-born Chinese read the English press. Refugee arrivals usually do, too, as they are likely to be educated, and consider Chinese papers here poorly written and too localized. This is the common plaint of new arrivals of all nationalities. They cannot—or won't—grasp the fact that American citizens, even of non-British ancestry, are more interested in the United States than in what is happening thousands of miles away. The newcomers have a point, though, in warning that America's survival may depend on these faraway occurrences.

The Chinese press, like our traditional smalltown paper, must keep close to its readers, who don't hesitate to criticise it and even go to the newsroom to see the editor and have it out with him. One complaint is that news of the Chinese mainland is held back as either too favorable or too unfavorable to the Reds. Most of the Chinese Americans have families on the mainland, and want to know the truth, good or bad. Another complaint is that the editor is too careful "not to offend the State Department" by failing to point out evidences of naivety or weakness in American policy—or lack of policy—that can deprive the captive peoples abroad of the hope they must retain if they are to gain their freedom.

These simple Chinese, especially the older, are less inclined than the younger or the intellectuals to be pessimistic. "What if Peking is strong today?" they ask. "We've had strong dynasties before. What happened to them? They've all been destroyed. What we want in China is a government that is both strong and right."

Simultaneously, there are subtle communist pressures, and some not subtle. Letters that arrive saying "You're not telling the truth," but are vague about what, are easy to spot as communist needling.

Editors and reporters, if anything, are put under heavier pressures than others in the community. Their relatives back on the Chinese mainland know no peace, if any still remain alive, or are known to the Peking regime. The tactic of intermittent periods of "leniency" and purge are the most dangerous. Names and information one hopefully or optimistically lets slip out, perhaps simply by addressing a letter, end up in the destruction of friends and loved ones unless one consents to "help the people," as agreement to join the Red underground is tactfully phrased.

The Chinese-language press has an additional handicap in adapting itself to local conditions. Because of the calculated elimination by the communists of Chinese culture and civilization on the mainland, and the rewriting of Chinese history, the Chinese press has the responsibility of helping to keep these national traits alive, through support of Free China, while adjusting to the American locale. This is an almost impossible dual task. Considerable financial sacrifice has been made by some overseas Chinese to help support Chinese-language papers that try to fulfill these patriotic demands.

Chinese editors in America have an advantage in that their readers generally live in crowded city areas, within easy, inexpensive reach of distributors. Readers in America frequently are older folk with poor eyesight. Many Chinese read the caligraphy only with difficulty. The type has to be large and bright. This means much less space, so the news has to be more compactly told. A Chinese-language paper in America may have only a quarter of the wordage of one in China.

The Chinese-language press has been unable to adjust itself to the new generation which is more at ease in English. There were four Chinese-language dailies in San Francisco at the start of 1960, but two collapsed in February. One was Kuo Min Yat Po (Chinese Daily Post), that began in 1927, and had 4,000 circulation. The Chinese World, the oldest Chinese paper in the United States, that started in 1891 in San Francisco, and has 9,000 circulation, had this to say editorially about its competitor's demise:

"As time goes on, we can expect younger generations of Chinese Americans to be less and less acquainted with their ancestral language. This means that even harder times are in store for Chinese newspapers.

"The Japanese newspapers face a similar problem. At one time in Hawaii, the Japanese community endeavored to solve the problem by urging people to subscribe, whether or not they were able to read Japanese. They hoped that by so doing it would permit Japanese-language newspapers to continue in existence and thus prevent a link with their ancestral culture and heritage from being snapped.

"A Japanese newspaper, many decades ago, initiated another move to adjust to changing times. This was the addition of an English section making it a bilingual paper. As far as Chinese papers are concerned, this development is still in its embryo stage and much work remains to be done. The main obstacles are the increased cost of new equipment and specialized labor. Apart from the bilingual trend, there seems to be no other course to pursue."

Lack of specialized labor is not the obstacle, for there are trustworthy journalists and printers of Chinese blood available, if a living wage were paid them.

The Chinese World itself is the only Chinese-language paper to publish anything in English, and this is a small portion of one page, started only seven years ago.

The collapse of the Chinese Daily Post eliminated the paper that had the closest ties on the West coast with the Kuomintang, the ruling party in Free China. Once before it had suspended, resuming publication only last March 15, but after nine months of struggle, again closed its doors. In the interim it had lost more than $20,000. Loss of operating capital and shortage of personnel forced the second suspension in two years.

The other daily to go out of existence was the Chinese World in New York, that also claimed 4,000 circulation. The venerable San Francisco paper of the same name started it in 1958.

All Chinese governments, from the Manchu Empire to the National Republic of China, and also the communist regime at Peking, have maintained the dual nationality concept. This is reflected in the Chinese-language press abroad. Anyone of Chinese blood is automatically considered a Chinese citizen. All living outside China are referred to as overseas Chinese, with no differentiation between an American of Chinese ancestry and a Chinese national on Taiwan or in Shanghai. Overseas Chinese delegates are members of Parliament at Taipei, the capital of Free China, while Red Peking picks amenable overseas Chinese as so-called people's delegates. Indeed, the communist regime has included all overseas Chinese, including those born in the United States or anywhere else abroad, in its census figure of 650,000,000 for the population of the so-called People's Republic of China.

The communist occupation of the mainland and the continuation of the war blocks normalization of conditions. Ties with the Kuomintang Party, as the operational wing of Free China, cannot be relaxed at this crucial time. Opposition parties never reached their full development on the mainland, and when the communists took over, were revealed overnight as riddled with Red agents. So, to an extent, was the Kuomintang, but it was able to revitalize itself on Taiwan. Under wartime conditions, to ask that a peacetime status be achieved in the multi-party system while the communists continue a constant barrage of shells and propaganda, is to ask the impossible. Until the mainland is freed, the political status quo is all that can be justifiably demanded; to ask more would be to insist that the Chinese be superhuman.

Dr. Sun Yat-sen, whose perseverance brought about the creation of the Chinese Republic, started the newspaper Young China at San Francisco in 1907, where it still is publishing, with a 5,500 circulation. Several who worked with the great, single-minded leader still are there.

The Chinese Times, with 9,500 circulation, also publishes at the Golden Gate. Americans of Chinese ancestry are its main supporters. While anti-communist, it tries to appear balanced regarding Taiwan, and centers its attention on what is happening in America. Significantly it is one of the most important papers, having the biggest West Coast circulation. In style, it is more a Cantonese paper than the others, although all more or less are of that order.

The largest circulation, 17,700, is claimed by a New York paper, the Chinese Journal, begun in 1928, which describes itself as: "The most progressive, intelligent and constructive Chinese daily in America." For years a Kuomintang organ, it lost so much money that New York Chinese bought it, put it back into the black, and gave it its own plant. The Chinese Journal sells well, too, in Philadelphia and Boston, and is still the closest to the Kuomintang on the East Coast.

Another outstanding daily is the China Tribune, boasting 10,000 circulation, that started in 1943, also with important Kuomintang links. Its editor is Y. Y. Pan, who came to the United States in 1949. He is a vigorous, bald-headed man of years, who was once president of the Shanghai City Council, and is a working journalist. He published the oldest Shanghai newspaper, the Shen Pao.

Under his editorship, the China Tribune makes a special appeal to Chinese students, with standards somewhat higher than the other papers. This way he is winning readers among the young Chinese and the scholars who left the mainland after its fall. He runs a weekly page of literature. Some of his old readers, understanding his goal, tell him patiently: "Your articles now are very good, I'm sure, and I congratulate you. But I don't understand them."

The China Tribune was established during the war by overseas Chinese in America. Many a laundryman and restaurateur bought stock in it. One of its editors later was accused of making a deal with Gen. Feng Yu-hsiang, the oversized, tragic figure who started

out as the "Christian General", performed a deed of
great merit by ending the hideous custom of binding
women's feet, was embroiled in Red conspiracy, and
died mysteriously in a shipwreck in the Soviet Arctic.
A subscribers' revolt brought in Pan along with others
who had fled the Reds, and they bought a part of
the stock. The paper changed its name in Chinese to
Chinese American Daily, but not its English title,
The China Tribune, in which it was registered.

2. THE NISEI PRESS

The most notable feature of the Japanese-language
press is that most of it—five dailies and one weekly—
is bilingual. There is good reason for the use of
English. More and more of its readers are American-
born, known as Nisei. When able to read Japanese
at all, they do so with difficulty, and frankly prefer
English. As second and sometimes third generation
American citizens, they absorb American traits with
the utmost facility. If it were not for the problems
created by race, they would not think of reading a
Japanese paper.

Their point of view could not have been more simply or concisely stated than it was by Nancy Fujita, a
college girl, in an essay contest conducted by the Japanese American Citizens' League and published in its
official English-language weekly, the Pacific Citizen,
which was begun in 1915 and has 6,500 circulation.
She wrote:

"I am an American youth of Japanese ancestry.
My heritage and physical features may distinguish me

from Americans of other extractions, but my beliefs
and behavior are truly those of an American.

"We Japanese Americans never have been un-
reasonable in our demands. We have never sought a
status of supremacy among other Americans; we have
only desired equality."

This recalled a wartime experience in Asia when
I was with the Office of Strategic Services. I needed
additional Japanese to write purportedly enemy newspapers and documents for behind-the-line distribution.
I put in an emergency call, and the Army responded
at once. As fast as a plane could travel, it brought
me a batch of fine fellows, Americans of Japanese
ancestry. They walked down the gangplank almost
rolling up their sleeves to start work.

The only trouble was that they could hardly read
or write Japanese. Their knowledge of it was on a par
with typical high school French.

The circulation figures of all Japanese-language
papers, bilingual or entirely in the old caligraphy,
show that they reach only a minority of those with
Japanese blood. The same situation prevails generally
in all minorities, as shown by comparison of circulation figures and population. The rest have gone over
to the English-language press. The overall circulation
of all Japanese periodicals for 1959 was 38,000. Yet
150,000 persons with Japanese blood live on the United
States mainland, 40,000 of them in Los Angeles.

In the bilingual papers, the English section occupies
about one-fourth of the space. Only the Pacific Citizen
and Crossroads, both weeklies put out in Los Angeles,
are all-English.

The Japanese press in America focusses mainly on our relations with Japan, and on what is of most influence on both countries. Exactly as the European-derived American looks eastward, and his sphere of interest is mainly the Atlantic Ocean and the nations that face it on both sides, the interest of these Japanese Americans of the West Coast is the Pacific Ocean, and the lands that abut it in both directions.

The New Japanese American News of Los Angeles, a bilingual daily, ran a first-page, two-column editorial by its special writer, Saburo Kido, in its Jan. 30, 1960 issue entitled "Observation." In it, he urged "persons of Japanese ancestry" to engage in a letter-writing campaign to friends, relatives and newspapers in Japan, urging ratification of the recently signed Security Pact with the United States. Kido was encouraged to start this drive, he wrote, by recollection of a similar one "which Americans of Italian ancestry carried on in a critical election campaign against the Communists a few years ago," which he said had the tacit encouragement of the State Department.

A headline over a first-page column in the Hokubei Mainichi the same day conveyed, in capsule form, the spirit of the Japanese American youth. It read: "Back Home From Japan." A fat tome could not summarize the checkered history of the Japanese American community more succinctly or dramatically. The Hokubei Mainichi, a bilingual daily of San Francisco that started in 1948, has 6,000 circulation. The article had for subtitle, "It's Nice and Quiet Here." Its author was William T. Kawai, who concluded:

"If you can but imagine the noise of one motor-cycle multiplied by hundreds lined three deep down a street, you will get a partial indication of the racket you encounter when you walk the streets of Tokyo . . . I wonder if Americans haven't become immune to the present accelerated type of living requiring a trans-plantation of the 'soul' to see not only the comparative difference, but to re-evaluate the human merits of a slower rat race. It's nice and quiet here."

The big switch to English was the solution reached by the Japanese-language publishers for their long-range problem of settling upon a formula that would retain Japanese Americans of later generations as sub-scribers. The English section helped the Japanese papers recover from the same wartime blow that shattered the German press.

The Japanese American community has shown itself flexible and alert. The shift to English began 35 years ago in San Francisco on the old Nichi Bei (Japan American News), which in 1921 was the larg-est of eleven Japanese-language dailies, with 12,000 circulation. Its closest competitor was another Golden Gate daily, the New World, with 10,000.

The late Kyutaro Abiko was then editor of Nichi Bei. The paper was liquidated in May of 1942, in its forty-fourth year, along with practically all Japanese publications, by the same bombs that rained down upon Pearl Harbor. The son, Y. W. Abiko, is now editor of Nichi Bei Times (Japanese American Times), begun in 1946 at San Francisco, which has amassed a 6,000 circulation.

Kyutaro Abiko started the first English-language section in the summer of 1925, allotting two columns, ten inches deep, to it. He went about it in a professional manner, bringing in a special editor, James A. B. Scherer, author of a number of books about Japan. The special section expanded until, just prior to our entry into World War II, it filled two of the paper's ten pages.

Other Japanese papers on the West Coast and in Hawaii began doing the same thing in the late 20s and early 30s, and an English section has been an integral part of nearly every Japanese newspaper since then.

"My father's original idea in starting an English section and securing Mr. Scherer as editor was to introduce Japanese culture, history and traditions to young Japanese Americans," Y. W. Abiko told me. "Since Japanese is a very difficult language to master, very few of the second generation Japanese know it well enough to read books, newspapers and magazines regularly.

"Because most subscribing families had children and young people interested in socials, sports, church and other news items, not only in their own community but in others, the English section became a necessary adjunct to Japanese papers."

The highest circulation claimed by the Japanese papers is 10,300 for the Rafu Shimo, a bilingual daily in Los Angeles, started in 1903. Denver has a Japanese daily, the Colorado Times, begun in 1914, 2,000 circulation. The New Japanese American News, begun in 1947, has 5,500.

The Japanese Americans do not have the many types of periodicals published by other minorities. Japanese American publications of all description number only ten. They have one religious semi-monthly, in addition to their newspapers. Popular and scholarly magazines published in Japan are of such a high order, and so easily available on the West Coast, that the need just does not arise for duplication.

Indeed, the excellent English-language dailies published in Japan, with airplane editions sent to the United States, present serious competition and keep the Japanese-language press in America on its toes. Nowhere else are American-style newspapers published abroad in English in such number and of so high a standard. Their comfortable circulations show that they exist in response to a genuine need, without depending upon official or artificial prodding.

Chapter Ten

The Communist Press

1. BY ITS OWN SCALES

The outright communist-language press is disarmingly small, with a commensurately slight circulation. Observers are inclined, therefore, to shrug these papers off as without influence, as if they lived by the same rules as ordinary newspapers. But they don't! Exactly as the Communist Party evaluates its membership, particularly when it has been purged down to its hard core, by other measurements, so must the importance of the communist press be gauged. The Party applies the same severe test to it, reducing it, too, to a hard core. "Sentimentalism" plays no part in it, nor any other "bourgeois" consideration, except as it lends itself to the zig-zag tactics which the Communists describe by such beguiling expressions as their "undulating line."

Communist papers are Party organs, their importance in the Party bearing no relation to normal factors that determine an ordinary newspaper's status. Their preferred location is strategic, in industrial areas vital to America's security. They exert their weight through contacts rather than circulation. A trusted agent in an industrial plant that would constitute a bottleneck in time of emergency is all the circulation that such a paper needs to fulfill its true function. The rest is screen.

As in all communist mechanism, the Red press has a long-range and a short-range program, and an overt and a covert set of objectives. These interlock along parallel lines of activity. One generally consists of propaganda pressure, the other is conspirational and operational. The former is well-known and visible enough not to require description here. This portion is supposed to detract attention from the other, that engages in Party activity generally that would not bear the light of day, including espionage, and co-ordinates the Red press with the rest of the communist network. This coordination is the secret weapon of communist effectiveness, with follow-through as its other big gun, two all-important factors which, by our default, they have practically to themselves.

This coordination is achieved by an intricate organizational pattern that passes along orders and money and relays secret reports and other information. A nationality group, with this as its responsibility, has been set up in almost every foreign-language community in America. This operates through a central headquarters linked directly with top Soviet Russian agents, through which all work is coordinated for home and abroad. Communist embassies and consulates have been brazenly used for such general staff activity, because of their internationally guaranteed immunity from inspection. Policy is smoothly synchronized this way, and coordinated with action, what China's fighting theoretician, Mao Tse-tung, calls "walking on both legs."

Details of how this mechanism operates have been provided by many firsthand sources, with such conclusive evidence that the Communist Party has been able to take refuge only in a dual tactic of vague, blanket denial, backstopped by every possible pressure to shut off discussion in the ordinary channels of communication, this hush-hush being its main defense. As a tactic, the party camouflages its trail by constantly changing road signs, giving its organizations and branches frequent new names, shaking up groups and re-arranging them in an equally confusing manner.

Responsibility in the foreign-language field was originally exercised by the International Workers Order, with headquarters in New York City, operating through many semi-autonomous sections strategically placed throughout the United States. Where the IWO was able to gain control of a respectable foreign-language fraternity by infiltration, it used this as its secret branch headquarters. Its tentacles sunk into numerous fellow traveler and so-called non-communist groups through its contacts with other communist intergroup organizations ranging from the American Slav Congress to an element in the Russian Orthodox Church that recognizes the authority of the Kremlin-controlled Moscow Patriarchate. Some of these associate groups present enough of a disarming front to be in fraternal relationship with some of our most trusted non-communist or even anti-communist organizations.

The Kremlin is able this way to pass a statement through these channels and then surface it in some completely trusted American outfit, as if the communists had nothing to do with it. The Kremlin then can pick it up again through Tass news agency with seeming innocence, attributing it to others. Action orders are issued the same way. This is known in psychological warfare as a "black" operation, while the term "gray" is applied to the intermediary, that is partly or wholly controlled in secret.

The IWO lost its name, and its duties were shuffled about in 1952, when its functions were exposed. An FBI operative named Mr. Matt Cvetic, who held high posts in the Red network, exposed its innermost secrets.

Communist leaders have given minute instructions concerning the role of the communist press as a weapon, in the literal sense of the word. Only the Soviet embassies and consulates, that operate behind a shield of diplomatic immunity, are in a more convenient position for operations than the Red press. The quasi-diplomatic status accorded to journalists and the special privileges they enjoy in a free society even puts them in some respects in a better position than diplomats, for they are unhindered by protocol, and have freer contact with all strata in society.

Many an alien in America, who has a loved one behind the Iron Curtain, has been interviewed by a so-called reporter for a foreign-language newspaper whose credentials they failed to look into, or who falsified his connections. The person interviewed may have casually referred, "off the record," to income received for special work, perhaps the translation of a book. A couple of months later, he receives a piteous letter from a mother or sister, or whoever happens to be living in the communist country, telling of some sudden new difficulty with the Red authorities over a ridiculous technicality. The letter mentions a fine imposed and pleads for this sum to be

sent, to avoid some horrible penalty, or to be released
from prison. By a revealing coincidence, this sum
usually is exactly the amount earned by the relative
in America. The interviewer had been a Red agent.
This is what happened to a Chinese lady this author
knew in Washington, soon after she was paid for a
writing assignment.

Communist functionaries, working as staff members and executives of a Red newspaper, travel freely at home and abroad. Their press card provides a
safe entry for communist activity. Their pathway is
cleared for them and protected from attack by the
American passport, their's for the simple asking, as
the result of a convenient Supreme Court decision and
the default of Congress. The State Department can
have a ream of incriminating documents about a
bogus journalist; no matter, he must be provided with
the open sesame of this invaluable United States passport, to use along with his press card, for Communist Party work abroad.

Communist newspapers in the United States differ fundamentally from others in the foreign-language
field, by all of them being alike. The non-communist
newspaper in each nationality group reflects the characteristics of its community. Its editor is more likely
to have his contacts on an English-language paper
than in another language group. Indeed, with few
exceptions, they rarely read the papers in other language groups. One has to go to the Red press to find
an interlocking relationship. The communist papers
are thoroughly coordinated.

Translate a Chinese, Polish or Lithuanian communist newspaper, and it is as alike to the others

in attitude and interpretation as peas in a pod; they're
all really the same paper, alike, too, to the English-
language Worker in New York or London, or any other
communist organ anywhere else, in Paris, Havana or
Jakarta. Identical tunes are pounded out in all, from
the same sheet music.

The communist press has conspirational depth,
penetrating into pink and even into anti-communist
papers, and into newspapermen's organizations, too.
The pink press is exploited the same as any fellow
traveler. The anti-Red papers in the foreign-language
field are infiltrated with or without management's
knowledge. These papers are the broken sad sacks.
They are always on the edge of bankruptcy. Their
vulnerability is in their advertising department.

A newspaper can obtain money for survival only
through three possible channels. One is direct support by a wealthy publisher or group of backers.
Newspapers are much too expensive for this, except
as a temporary expedient, with the expectation of re-
couping all or most of the money later on. The de-
ficits of opinion magazines are covered this way. They
have never made ends meet.

Another channel is subsidy by an organization,
government bureau or other outside medium. A return is always expected for such expenditure. When
it isn't financial, it has to do with influencing people's
minds. When the source or the motive cannot be disclosed without arousing an adverse reaction, it means
that the aim is propaganda in its colloquial, derogatory
sense; it is corruption of the press.

The third channel is through advertising, the traditional means by which the American press supports

itself free from government or other vested control. We have found that this works out successfully when reinforced by separate handling of news and advertising, and their clear demarcation in the paper. Our radio and television found themselves on a dead end street through failure to observe this technique, allowing their advertisers to do the programming, abdicating what they had no right to abandon, their complete responsibility for content, by failing to insist on the separate handling of programs and commercials all down the line. Fashion magazines that do retailing through their articles, in collaboration with advertisers, are able to get away with it because they have kept away from political content.

Foreign-language papers, chronically sick financially, live from hand to mouth, and are pathetically underequipped and understaffed. They generally lack the most important red corpuscles that go into a paper's bloodstream, national advertising. Small ads obtained locally hardly cover the cost of type-setting, and are expensive to solicit.

Numerous advertisements by travel agencies and firms that ship relief packages are a conspicuous feature of the foreign-language papers, principally the Slavic. The source of this advertising is very often behind the iron curtain. American importers of merchandise from the Red bloc countries rarely place their orders direct. They operate through a few American agencies. Beer, canned stews, dumplings and other delicacies, which the people of communist countries themselves frequently lack, are exported by the Red governments. Polish hams were being advertised for sale in the United States when there was an unprecedented meat famine in Poland.

An advertising executive of a foreign-language paper told me his experience in soliciting such ads. His paper has unchallengeable advantages which he explained to the American agent. "I know all this well enough," the latter replied. "But didn't your paper run an editorial about the meat shortage in Poland?" He made it plain that his clients would not allow their ads to appear in papers that published such news. As if showing his broadmindedness, he went on to say that he was sure they didn't expect pro-communist news to be published. "Only not that sort of news! Do you really have to run it?" he inquired, as if selectivity could not constitute just as much falsification as an outright lie.

My friend, who obviously didn't get the account, walked over to his newspaper rack and brought over one of the papers that did. Once it, too, had run all the news. Now news unfavorable to the communists on such matters simply doesn't appear.

On another foreign-language paper, someone generally known as a "communist money man" is employed as an advertising solicitor. The paper runs anti-communist editorials. But its news columns now no longer run all the news. The space that formerly went to information the communist bloc doesn't like is now filled with travel and relief package advertisements. The paper was virtually being supported by them.

Another singular factor about such advertising is that it quite frequently provides the excuse for someone on the paper to make a special trip to Europe. The agency suddenly no longer suffices, and a personal contact has to be made. People in the newspaper business know well enough that advertising does not pay for such travel. The Communists use these accounts, and the business they drum up, as a channel for the transfer of money, and for other party missions.

2. DOCUMENTATION

A graphic description of how the communists operate their foreign-language press network was provided by John Lautner, who was a trained leader in it until a grim comedy of intra-Party blunders and recriminations, leading to his brutal kangaroo trial, led him to quit communism in disillusioned disgust. Lautner related his experiences before various government bodies, one of which was the House Committee on Un-American Activities, on March 12, 1957.

Lautner, who died recently, was of Hungarian derivation.] late in 1929 in New York, was sent to a training school of its Hungarian section, then was named district secretary of the Party's Nationality Bureau in Michigan. From there he was transferred to a similar post in Canada where, in addition, he was made editor of a weekly. His next transfer was to the same duties in Cleveland, where he became editor of a Hungarian-language daily. He went up the communist ladder slowly, in 1941 being appointed head of the Party's National Hungarian Bureau. Some months later, he headed the Hungarian section of the IWO, from where he went into the Army, receiving Intelligence training and being assigned to psychological warfare in the Mediterranean.

After being demobilized in June, 1945, he was re-appointed national secretary of the Hungarian Bureau and put on the Party's Nationality Groups Commission.

Richard Arens, staff director of the House Un-American Activities Committee, asked him why the Party put such emphasis on foreign language groups in the United States. Lautner explained that the objective was "basic industry—like steel, mining, packing, auto, etc. There is where you find a large section of the nationality groups in these industries. Therefore, from the point of view of the Communist Party it was extremely important to influence through the nationality groups and their language papers these segments of the working class because it was essential to win the support of these workers for the program and activities of the Communist Party." The following interrogation then took place:

Mr. Lautner: "The Communist Party through the Nationality Groups Commission gave leadership and guidance to the various nationality group bureaus that were responsible for publications. For example, in the Hungarian field we had the Hungarian Daily Journal after 1945, which had at that time about 7,000 circulation. The main readership came from the industrial segment of American life, and the paper tried to play an important role in reflecting the party policies and party program and party activities through this publication.

"It was the same situation with the other papers. The National Bureau secretaries were invited to Party gatherings, to Nationality Commission meetings. Editors were invited by members of the political committee of the Party where they were briefed on how best to put forward the Party line as to the Party day-to-day activities and how to reflect that best in their various newspapers. If we speak of control, it was that kind of a control."

Mr. Arens: "What was the relationship between the International Workers Order and the Communist foreign-language press during your experience?"

Mr. Lautner: "My first acquaintance with the IWO came somewhere in 1932, when I came back from Canada, when various national group sections began to join it. I was at the Chicago convention. I think it was in 1932 or 1933. All I remember is that the Chicago fair was going on at the time. The following resolution was voted by the Hungarian section here. Besides being part of the International Workers Order, the membership—the section itself—will tax the membership 10 cents per member, a so-called press tax. That 10 cents per each member was divided into 8 cents for the Hungarian Communist paper at that time, and 2 cents for the Daily Worker.

"I think other sections of the IWO followed the same routine by taxing their members press taxes at that time. Their respective papers got 8 cents—and 2 cents went to the Daily Worker. Besides that, there was other financial support to the language press and the Daily Worker in the form of full-page advertise-

ments and greetings on numerous occasions in the
Daily Worker.

"Besides that, the readership in the main for these
language papers came from the membership of the
IWO. For example, I know in the Hungarian section
another source of revenue was to print the full minutes
of the executive committee meeting of the Hungarian
section of the IWO for which there was a considerable
payment made to the newspaper. Readership and financial support came from the IWO.

"In addition to that, IWO members in many parts
of the country, particularly in the larger cities, went
out in campaigns to gain new subscribers for their
respective communist language newspapers. There
was a very close working relationship between the
language papers and the IWO and that relationship
was always encouraged by the Nationality Groups
Commission of the Communist Party itself. That is
the type of relationship the Party wanted."

Mr. Arens: "Is there such a thing as a pipeline
for directives from Moscow to the foreign-language
press in the United States?"

Mr. Lautner: "Directives do come and did come
in various forms. There is not one pipeline. There are
all sorts of methods employed. In the case of the
Communist International, the congresses established
the tactical line for the Parties to follow. These tactical lines were printed in publications like the Communist International and the Inprecorr, the International Press Correspondence, and other publications.
Here the Party, as I stated before, made it its business to sit down with the nationality group bureaus

and editors of these newspapers and through conferences saw to it that the Party line was properly reflected in these language papers."

"The Nationality Groups Commission, previously known as the language department of the Party, made a survey and study of these language newspapers from time to time to see how they reflected the Party line in the newspapers."

Gordon H. Scherer, Representative from Ohio, then asked: "Did these practices about which you are telling us continue up to the time that you left the Party in 1950?"

Mr. Lautner: "Yes. After 1945 it took a different form. When the Communist International Bureau was established in 1947, the official organ of the Communist Information Bureau was a weekly newspaper called 'For a Lasting Peace, For a People's Democracy'. That reflected the international line, so to speak—the thinking of the international leaderships, such as the report to the Warsaw Conference that laid down the fundamental tactical task for a coming period after the formation of the Cominform— this found its way in the channels of propaganda to the party presses over here through various methods— through consultations, conferences, and the Nationality Groups Commissions had meetings."

Mr. Arens: "During the course of your experience, were the communist editors under discipline to put the Communist Party line in the publications which they edited?"

Mr. Lautner: "Yes . . . discipline came from two directions, first from above. If the Party line was

not followed the person speaking for that line in the
paper was severely reprimanded, and if necessary,
removed. That happened, too. Also, there is a severe
criticism and sometimes asking for discipline from
below, from various committees in various cities that
criticize the paper. Their critical evaluation is needed also at times by the editor. So it comes from two
different sources."

One of the anomalies of the cold-hot war is the
vast amount of firsthand, highly-documented, irre-
futable and exclusive material gathered by House and
Senate Committees, printed in booklet form at tax-
payer's expense and made available to all for the asking, free or at a nominal price. They hardly reach
the American voter. He learns next to nothing about
them. They are next to ignored by the daily press
and by our educational institutions. Such initial publicity as is given is usually uninformatively brief,
hidden in some inside corner, or based upon some
secondary point or irrelevant issue that skirts around
the real disclosures. Then a hush descends on these
publications. Here and there they are filed away,
usually unread. Yet they deal conclusively with matters of decisive importance to America's stability,
security and survival, and frequently contain undeniable material unobtainable elsewhere.

Meanwhile, editorial writers, columnists and professors complain that students and the public generally are not being taught about the dangers of communism, and ask how they can possibly be expected
to fight it without understanding what it is, how it
operates, and what its successes and failures have

been in penetrating our society. Yet these same writers, professors and institutions are receiving all this vast amount of material that has been patiently and sometimes dangerously gathered, giving exactly the background they ask. They file it away on dusty shelves or in deep wastebackets, rarely read.

The result is that, by a process of elimination, what is told in answer to this earnest appeal for information, is what the fellow traveler and even the Communist want to put across.

The findings on communism by the various government bodies are practically a taboo subject in a large sector of our communications channels and educational circles. How this arose will some day, if a Pearl Harbor sputnik in the interval doesn't make the whole subject purely academic, be an essay theme for many a university degree.

Knowledge of the facts would lead many a person, who is on record minimizing these issues, to change his position drastically. Many use every possible excuse to avoid facing the inconvenient facts. This psychological gimmick explains how so many weak-willed but otherwise fine persons allow themselves, by default, to be used as pawns.

Thus it has been, for instance, as regards both the foreign-language press published in America and foreign publications pouring into the United States. Each year, literally millions of tons of such propaganda newspapers and other propaganda periodicals, all communist, enter the United States through the mails from behind the iron and bamboo curtains. Additional fantastic amounts are shipped to us by way of neutralist or friendly countries. The ramifications of this are so enormous, including its effect on our security, that it requires separate analysis at a later date.

Part of this problem is the transshipment by mail, going on all the time, of untabulated thousands of tons of communist publications through the United States, principally at New Orleans, from Mexico to all of Central and South America. The most inflammatory anti-American material is contained in this propaganda. By another of those legalistic bottlenecks which we appear incapable of breaking through nowadays, the American public even helps pay the transportation costs of this pro-Moscow incitation to Latin America to throw over its United States ties and join the Soviet Bloc.

Few persons have the least inkling of any of this, all of which is dovetailed in with the products of communist publications in the United States.

As far back as August 17, 1951, Nathan B. Lenvin, Assistant Chief, Internal Security and Foreign Agents Registration Section in the Criminal Department of the Justice Department, told a Senate Subcommittee:

"In the organizational structure of the Communist Party they have set up what are known today as foreign-language commissions, the function of each commission and its primary purpose being to work among the foreign element in the United States to which the particular language commission belongs. Each of these language commissions has its own publication. For example, there is a Jewish publication, an

Italian publication, a Russian publication, an Hungarian publication, and so forth."

Mr. Arens, then staff director of this Subcommittee asked: "All of which are Communist publications; is that correct?"

Mr. Lenvin: "All of which are Communist publications, and which, of course, consistently follow the Communist Party line."

The communist foreign-language press was dealt a blow about five years ago when deportation proceedings were begun against a number of editors illegally in the United States. Those concerned included Russky Golos, Russian; Tyomies-Eteenpain, Finnish; Morgen Freiheit, Jewish-language, and Uus Ilm (New World), of New York, Estonian, now a monthly claiming a few hundred circulation.

One of the slyest gimmicks of the communist foreign-language press is its dissemination of fabricated news purporting to come from neutralist and other foreign countries. A behind-the-scenes explanation of how this is done was given by Aleksandr Y. Kasnakheyev, a man who helped do it until he defected from Soviet intelligence. He was engaged in Red psychological warfare while attached to the Soviet Embassy in Rangoon, Burma. Appearing before the Senate Internal Security Subcommittee on Dec. 14, 1959, under questioning by Julien G. Sourwine, chief counsel, he declared: "One of my assignments with the Intelligence Service was the work with usage of Burmese press for Communist aims. Soviet intelligence regularly published in different Burmese publications provocative anti-American and anti-West articles. These articles were fabricated in Moscow, in

KGB (Committee of State Security) headquarters, sent to Burma on microfilms, then developed in Soviet Embassy. One intelligence officer was translating the text from Russian into English. Another officer was planting this material in Burmese press."

Mr. Sourwine: "When you say translated into English—"

Mr. Kasnakheyev: "From Russian into English. I know this because sometimes—"

Mr. Sourwine: "Is the Burmese press printed in English?"

Mr. Kasnakheyev: "No. They translate—when these articles were given to KGB-controlled Burmese press, they translated them from English into Burmese. In the next stage, when this article appeared in Burmese newspapers, it was my duty to check the Burmese text against Russian text, and then my corrections and corrected text were sent back to Moscow through Tass agency. Then it was distributed. Then Tass agency distributed this material, now as a true story, published in the press throughout the world, especially in countries of special interest."

Mr. Kasnakheyev either participated in or witnessed the use of the press this way for clandestine warfare, under the direction of Ivan Vozniy, KGB chief in Burma, who had the rank of Colonel of State Security. Two articles were planted in the Mirror, a communist-controlled paper in Rangoon, at the height of the 1958 anti-Red revolt in Indonesia. As Kasnakheyev tells it in the New Leader magazine of Jan. 18, 1960:

"One of the articles reproduced a letter, purportedly from an Indonesian rebel leader named

Sjamsuddin to the American Ambassador in Toyko. The other purported to be from 'Admiral Frost' of the U. S. Navy to another Indonesian rebel leader. At Vozniy's direction, I translated both of these 'letters' from the Russian-language photocopies into English, and later checked the articles published in the Burmese-language Mirror against the original Russian photocopies. The Sjamsuddin 'letter' was dated March 15, 1958, but was published in the Mirror in May. In it, Sjammudin asked the U. S. Ambassador for help and talked of aid for the rebellion from the Southeast Asian Treaty Organization. The Frost 'letter', which was published in the Mirror in early June, advised the rebels not to surrender and stated that the U. S. would continue to help them. These articles were signed by the Mirror's 'Special Correspondent in Djakarta'. These Rangoon articles were then distributed among the Indonesian political circles, played up in the world communist press and even republished in an Indonesian-language newspaper, the Bintang Timur, which was also controlled by Soviet intelligence."

Mr. Kasnakheyev named some of the papers in various Southeast Asian countries that he knew from his own experience were being used this way by "the large Soviet press network." He listed Blitz of Bombay and the Times of Delhi, both much-quoted Indian papers, La Patrie in Thailand and Bintang Timur in Indonesia.

While perpetrating these frauds on one side, on the other side the communist mechanism smears papers that are favorable to the Free World by accusing them of being bribed by the United States. This also achieves a diversionary end, and tends to neutralize disclosures of Red complicity by providing the so-called liberal excuse that "both sides" are doing the same thing, so why blame Moscow and Peking?

The Tass correspondent in Rangoon, named Kovtu-nenko, ran a dispatch early in 1959, purportedly from India, declaring that three Burmese newspapers, the Nation, Guardian and Reporter, were used by the American Embassy to undermine Burma's policy of neutrality.

"This article was written in Moscow originally, planted in the Delhi Times, and signed by their non-existent Rangoon correspondent," Mr. Kasnakheyev wrote in the New Leader. "The article was then sent to Rangoon for distribution through Tass channels. In this case, the Soviet propaganda machine did not work well and a definite mistake was made in the last link of the chain. The channel of distribution was not properly selected, and the editor of the Nation sued Kovtunenko for defamation of character. Kov-tunenko hid out in the Soviet Embassy, to escape trial. As far as I know, he is still afraid to come out."

Communist papers everywhere, such as those in the foreign-language field in the United States, are utilized in initiating and propagating such false news. Much of the anti-American material and incitation to anti-American demonstrations that purportedly ema-nate spontaneously everywhere from Cuba to Egypt, from Japan to Italy, is concocted through this simple exploitation of newspaper technique.

In every foreign-language community, the com-munist paper is on the alert to print such inflammatory information involving the United States and the particular nationality at which the Red organ is aimed. Maximum impact can be expected this way in this behind-the-lines propaganda warfare. Communism considers itself, from the long-range, dialectical materialist viewpoint, in a state of war in non-communist countries, regardless what peaceful objectives might be proclaimed in pursuance of a short-range, tactical goal. This double-barreled approach gives the Red hierarchy the same advantage that the United States military would have had if we could have secretly edited a newspaper in Berlin or Toyko during World War II.

At a hearing on March 15, 1957, this exchange took place with David S. Krinkin, identified as editor of Russky Golos, concerning an article it published blaming "American intervention" for the catastrophe in Hungary:

Mr. Arens: "Is that a true and correct translation?"

Mr. Krinklin: "The translation is true."

Mr. Arens: "Did you write this?"

Mr. Krinklin: "No."

Mr. Arens: "Who wrote it?"

Mr. Krinklin: "This I decline to answer on the Fifth Amendment."

Mr. Arens: "Was it written under your supervision?"

Mr. Krinklin: "I decline to answer."

Mr. Arens: "Was it written in Moscow and then put in your paper here?"

Mr. Krinklin: "I decline to answer this on the Fifth Amendment."

William P. Rogers, government attorney general, in a report to Congress in May, 1958, on the workings of the Foreign Agents Registration Act, wrote: "In June, 1956, a two-count indictment was returned by a Federal Grand Jury sitting in Detroit, Mich., against the Romanian-American Publishing Association and its officers, wherein it was charged that the Association unlawfully and wilfully acted as an agent of the Government of the People's Republic of Romania without having filed the registration statement required by the Act. The officers were charged with unlawfully failing to cause the organization to register. On February 26, 1958, Judge Frank A. Picard in the Federal District Court in Detroit imposed a fine of $2,000 upon the Publishing Association following its plea of nolo contendere to the indictment. Prior to the acceptance of the plea, the Association had executed and filed the required registration statement.

"The Association, which publishes a weekly Romanian language newspaper called 'Romanul-American' had been charged with acting as a publicity and propaganda agent for the Romanian Ministry of Cultural Affairs."

If one were to read the controlled press in all the Red Bloc countries, it would appear that the most influential and largest circulating newspapers in America were those Red rags that comparatively few ever see, even in large nationality groups. They are quoted exhaustively to give the impression that the American public and government accept communism as unbeatable, and that any hope the peoples of the Red-dominated lands might have of Free World help will turn to ashes when put to the test. The unhappy example of Hungary and Tibet are constantly rubbed into them. These papers are the only ones permitted to circulate. In a cynical interpretation of cultural exchange, this communist press is presented as representative of American thinking. Even if these communist sheets had no circulation, this use of them alone would make them very valuable to the party's world apparatus.

Advertising is a highly expensive proposition when one tackles a newspaper such as the New York Times. The regular foreign-language press has no money for this or any other institutional, much less political advertising. The communist newspapers, appraised from any legitimate basis, cannot possibly consider such an expenditure. What is self-evident is that the money for any such advertising that does appear would have to come through clandestine channels, whatever the front may be.

On February 16, 1960, an advertisement filling two-thirds of a page appeared in the New York Times, signed: "Armenian Herald, Estonian Monthly, Hungarian World, Polish 'Glos Ludowy,' Russian 'Russky Golos,' Ukrainian News, Lithuanian 'Laisve'." This was not a commercial advertisement; it was entirely political. Entitled "An Appeal to the President of the United States", it supported the Kremlin all down the line against the United States on the crucial issue of disarmament, in which Moscow was trying to maneuver Washington into an agreement that would remove our defenses while leaving the usual loopholes for the Reds to go ahead and build up all the nuclear strength they can. This particular advertisement had to do with what was possibly the most fateful negotiation of all time. The Red press in the United States, along with such collaborators as it can obtain, was proceeding as customary, in the manner of a military detachment that had seized a position inside the enemy's lines, and exploited it for all it was worth. The Nazi troops did this in the Battle of the Bulge, putting on American uniforms. Any claim that this was just an ordinary advertisement would be tantamount to a directive being issued at the Battle of the Bulge ordering no defense to be made against the infiltrated enemy force because its men were wearing American uniforms. This is the unrealistic position we take time and time again on such matters.

The legitimate nationality organizations in the foreign-language field at once denounced the advertisement, but of course lacked the money to pay for any such advertisement in reply. They included the Assembly of Captive European Nations, the Conference of American Citizens of Central and Eastern European Descent, the Polish American Congress, the Ukrainian Congress and the Federation of Hungarian Former Political Prisoners.

The overwhelming majority of the foreign-language papers in America have no connection with the Communist Party, and the bulk of them are anti-communist. Readers of this particular advertisement would have no way of knowing, unless the newspaper had seen fit to editorially tell them so, that this was one of the most brazen pieces of Communist Party propaganda that could be foisted on the American public.

The columnist, David Lawrence, wrote: "What is important to know is where some of the publications with Communist sympathies get their money. Spokesmen for refugee organizations say that much of it is collected from residents of this country who are subjected to a kind of blackmail. Unless, for instance, they deposit money with packages of food and clothing that they wish to send to relatives behind the iron curtain, these packages may not be delivered abroad.

"The money, it is now charged, is being used to pay for propaganda of all kinds, no small part of which is designed to scare Americans out of their wits about the dangers of radioactive 'fallout'."

The travel and relief package advertising accounts, exploited as a Red propaganda pressure against our foreign-language papers, is part of this "black" operation by the Moscow-Peking Axis in its psychological war against the Free World, with the United States its principal target.

The Hungarian World listed in the advertisement was actually Amerikai Magyar Szo (Hungarian-American Word), a New York weekly begun in 1952, which claims a 3,000 circulation, four of whose staff officers took the Fifth Amendment in 1957 when asked if they were Communist Party members by the House Un-American Activities Committee. This paper specializes in glamorizing news of life in Red Hungary. One of its favorite artifices is to quote the New York Times, always selecting points that uphold the communist viewpoint. The paper is a study in double-talk. Another of its favorite tricks is to play up whatever news it can obtain of any difficulties in which any Hungarian freedom fighter who took refuge in the United States might find himself. These carefully selected stories add up to a portrait of a most unhappy United States, contrasted with the supposed joys that the Hungarian refugees left behind them. When a Hungarian freedom fighter committed suicide in Detroit, the paper said this would not have happened if he had only stayed at home. Such articles have to be read in connection with their companion pieces in the redefection papers sent into the United States in Hungarian and other languages from East Germany for their full impact to be appreciated.

The editor of Glos Ludowy, Polish, similarly invoked the Fifth Amendment at the same hearings. The editor and secretary of Russky Golos went through the same act, and so did the editor of Ukrainski Visti (Ukrainian News), that was started in New York in 1920, and claims 2,200 circulation.

Glos Ludowy also won notoriety for the brazenness of Joseph Kowalski, its editor for years. Benjamin Gitlow, who was formerly high in Communist Party circles in America, identified Kowalski as a Red operator. Kowalski then requested deportation to Soviet Russia, but some time later was discovered back in the United States, on a mission for Moscow.

The American goverment ordered him deported once more, but Moscow promptly took advantage of a gap in American law by simply refusing to take him back. Under a Supreme Court decision, Kowalski was now freed to pursue whatever mission the Red network had given him. Every effort in Congress to deal with this fantastic situation has been frustrated, making a dangerous farce of American jurisprudence and its security both.

Laisve (Freedom) is a semi-weekly put out in Richmond Hill, New York, that started in 1911 and claims 5,100 circulation. Other Lithuanian papers have exposed its whitewashing of communist excesses in Lithuania, and the rosy picture of conditions presented by its editor after expensive trips behind the iron curtain. Naujienos (Lithuanian Daily News) of Chicago, a reputable daily started in 1943, 43,250 circulation, printed letters from Lithuania refuting Laisve.

The Red papers, in signing their names in somewhat garbled form in English in an advertisement that appeared in a major New York newspaper, could assume that its readers would certainly not have heard of these Congressional hearings and would not know about the incrimination of their editors. The details had received little or no notice in the press.

Readers of the advertisement could not know, therefore, that this was the same Laisve whose editor appeared in a Congressional hearing on March 15, 1957 and took the Fifth Amendment on the question whether he was a member "of the Communist conspiracy" when naturalized. As editor, during the Korean War, his paper accused the United States of massacring prisoners of war on the island of Koje, Korea, picking up communist slander as gospel truth.

At the time of the inquiry that unmasked the perpetrators of the Katyn Massacre, his paper wrote: "All this 'investigation' is nothing but a farce" by those who "favor hangman and Nazis." The revelations of persecution of Jews in the Soviet Union were similarly refuted.

The editor then, who took the Fifth Amendment repeatedly, was Roy Mizara. The editor at the time of the bland advertisement was still Roy Mizara.

Chapter Eleven

Where We Stand Now

1. THE UKRAINIANS AND MR. CHYZ

A walking encyclopedia of the foreign-language press in America passed away with the death on Dec. 13, 1958, of Yaroslav J. Chyz. He carried volumes of data in his head, that he had gathered as a foreign-language journalist and as a writer and consultant on the subject for decades. He headed the Foreign Language Press Division of the Common Council from 1942 until his end. Of Western Ukrainian derivation, he came to the United States in 1922, becoming a citizen seven years later.

In an article he published in the Council's magazine, Common Ground, in its spring, 1943 issue, he pleaded that heed be paid to the reports of the foreign-language editors who had cast their lot with the United States, pointing out that "one or another of their newspapers saw and pointed out the various danger spots in the world long before the general American press became aware of them." Some of his statements in this 1943 article read as if they referred to events 16 or 17 years later.

"The Lithuanian, the Estonian, and the Latvian American editor is not as lucky as the Polish and Yugoslav," he wrote. "In some Victory Parades their people have not been allowed to carry the flags of their native countries because that might offend the Soviet

Union. They have been told to 'lay low' and keep quiet . . . "

He might have been referring to Washington's preparations for Premier Khrushchev's reception. Foreign-language editors seemed to paraphrase, in a 1959 context, the question in this 1943 article by Mr. Chyz: "From his inside knowledge of a particular country or situation he (the foreign-language editor) may feel that United Nations policy is questionable or sometimes even dangerous to a lasting peace in the postwar period. Is he to speak? Is he to keep silent?"

Practically every blunder and misfortune that has befallen the Free World has been the subject of warning in the foreign-language press, sometimes backed up by exclusive details from the spot. An anti-American item planted by the communist network in a Hong Kong paper has more chance of reaching the American public. Yet, as Mr. Chyz pointed out: "As a body, the editors of the American foreign-language press have been, and to a certain degree still are, one of the best informed groups on world affairs in this country."

"In fact," Mr. Chyz wrote in his prophetic piece, "it might be a great help to ultimate American unity and the clarification of postwar aims if the English press would pay closer attention to the foreign-language press and get more seriously interested in matters and issues discussed there, which are not so much 'stew in the melting pot' as warning grumblings of serious explosions of much concern to America. It would help both ways: the foreign-language press would see situations in the mirror of the English press in more objective perspective. And the English-language writers would learn that Americans of Polish, Croatian, Serbian, Slovak, Czech, Hungarian, and other descents are interested in European issues not so much because Hodza, Matuszewski, Eckhardt, Subotich, or others 'stir them up,' but often because they see better the possible dangers in the European situation. They want things after this war settled so their youngsters will not have to go abroad again to correct with blood mistakes and blunders born out of ignorance or lack of proper understanding."

This, when read today, makes one shudder, it is so timely.

He went on: "They want Hitler out, but they do not think that occupation by Stalin will be much of a change to their people in Europe. But to say so in their papers, to advocate a policy which would offend our Russian ally, is not easy. It may even be dangerous."

Replace the name of Stalin with Khrushchev's and he is referring to present-day "co-existence." These editors understand how fundamentally the word differs in communist language from the English.

"Many an editor," Mr. Chyz wrote, "must avoid some of these issues, must tone them down, or satisfy himself with platitudes, although he knows well that the problem is a possible danger spot or breeding place of some future war and a potential threat to American lives."

He was editor-in-chief for years of Narodna Volya (The People's Will), a Ukrainian newspaper in Scranton, Pa., begun in 1911, then a tri-weekly and now a bilingual weekly with 7,500 circulation. His Ukrainian American community now has two dailies, Svoboda (Liberty), of Jersey City, N. J., begun in 1893, with a 20,100 circulation, and Ameryka (America), of Philadelphia, that started in 1913, 10,000 distribution.

Mr. Chyz knew the face of the enemy.

At a hearing March 10, 1957, Michael Tkach, identified as editor of the Ukrainian Daily News, New York City, was asked by Mr. Arens: "Did you have knowledge of activities in this country of the Russian secret police?" After conferring with his counsel, Tkach replied: "Fifth Amendment I invoke."

He was the man whom, on May 13, 1949, a newspaper witness, Elizabeth Bentley, testified: "In addition to his duties as being head of the Ukrainian Daily News, he was working with the Russian secret police . . . He found other agents for us among the Ukrainians in this country."

The new testimony brought out that under his continued editorship—during the Korean War—his paper accused the United States of germ warfare, declaring in the May 7, 1952 issue that our denial "does not convince anybody." The paper branded the Hungarian Freedom Revolt a Fascist plot, and gloated over its suppression as a lesson to the satellite lands that to follow Free World urgings "leads them to dead end, toward ruin and destruction."

This calculated destruction of Ukrainian personality by the Kremlin is reflected in the overall increase in readers of anti-communist Ukrainian-language publications of all types, reversing the trend in most other nationality groups. The Ukrainians are among our most active American foreign-language elements.

In the 52 years between 1886 and 1938, Ukrainians published 135 newspapers in the United States, including six dailies, four bi-weeklies or tri-weeklies, and 36 weeklies. In 1938 they had two dailies, two tri-week-lies, two bi-weeklies and ten weeklies.

The first Ukrainian paper, Ameryka, was pub-lished in 1886 at Shenandoah, Pa., a bi-monthly orig-inally, becoming a weekly within a year.

2.   UNFINISHED BUSINESS

Our forefathers never could have imagined, in their most hopeful dreams, the prosperity and greatness that would come in a few generations to the communi-ties they founded, many at that time more inaccessible from each other than almost any two cities on the globe today. They certainly would never have con-ceived, in their most imaginative moments, the type of problems which have accompanied this staggering growth.

Not since Athens had such extraordinary talent and actual genius been gathered together in any one locale anywhere on earth. The American Constitution that they thought up, and the body of customs and laws with which they buttressed it, stand to this day as a monument to their greatness. Their creation of a government of check and balance has never been sur-passed. So long as it can be maintained, dictatorship of any type is impossible. The check and balance sys-tem they gave to politics in 1789 is an modern as the flexibility which a Twentieth Century engineer gives to a bridge so it can withstand the mightiest hurricane. These concepts of our forefathers remain eternally modern because they were based on timeless truths. Understandably, therefore, the Constitution is the only document of that day still in force anywhere on earth.

This is what has given the United States the stamina to take in stride revolutionary buffeting in all spheres of social and political life. The admission to statehood of Alaska and Hawaii, giving these distant territories a status equal in every legal respect to that of California and Virginia, was one such fundamental change, and it certified for all the world to see that the United States is now irrevocably and permanently a global power, something the rest of the world probably saw coming before we did. Isolationist nostalgia can achieve little in the face of one of our states now being located plumb in the middle of the vast Pacific Ocean, and another way up by the North Pole. In keeping with this trend, Puerto Rico has now begun to hammer at our gateway for a grant of similar status. Whether this is the conclusion of a momentous chapter in our history, or the start of a new one only the future will tell, and this will depend on the degree of adventuresomeness and creativity that we still possess.

In language and in outlook, Hawaii and Alaska are practically like our mainland, or fast becoming so. Puerto Rico still is looking in two directions, pulled by the Spanish language. The future, too, will have to work out this dilemma.

The expression, "melting pot," has almost dropped out of our language. Only a few decades ago, it was our proudest label. The words "liberal" and "objectivity" and "tolerance" had different connotations then, too. Changes have quietly come over many of our basic words.

Liberal, objective, tolerant then indicated an open mind toward all points of view, without restricting them to any specific number, whereas nowadays there is an assumption that there must be two sides to every issue, two points of view offered, practically always two. Two is convenient for radio and television forums, and fits neatly into titles for forums and discussion groups. One or the other—this is the principle of the mechanical brain, too, the piece of plastic or cardboard that slowly is being given the role of appraiser as well as calculator. More and more nowadays, it makes the choice for us.

This dualist approach is definitely part of communist ideology, which declares that there is no middle road; that it is either one or the other, entirely, with no alternative or modification possible.

We once had a definite reason for "seeing all sides," which was to facilitate a process of elimination and choice, in order to reach a decision, in order to make up one's mind definitely on what was the best course, the best purchase, or the best anything. One made up one's mind, that was the point, and then one acted accordingly. One took an action. This doing was the objective.

The way it works out nowadays is that one is rebuked for being "subjective" or "intolerant" if he goes through this process in order to reach a decision between conflicting points of view or diverse procedures. We proceed as if, in order to keep the show going, two sides have to be artificially maintained on all questions and all issues at all times. Instead of decision, we reach permanent indecision, in a state of perpetual confusion, creating a system of chaos on the premise that this is what is meant by being democratic. We only have to read our newspapers and listen to the usual speeches to find out that our words are being given altered or opposite meanings, in the manner of the fictional Newspeak of George Orwell, or the dialectical materialist vocabulary of the Marxists.

Yet it should be evident to the most casual observer that the destiny of the United States will be determined by the manner in which we define our words. A word is something specific, like friendship or hate, hot or cold, sitting or walking. Lukewarm feelings, like lukewarm water, are specifics, too. An American is a type of human being with great flexibility, but there is a limit beyond which he is no longer American. A whole assortment of factors enter into making him an American. The type is not unchangeable, either; we are constantly modifying our outlook. But there remains an underlying point of view and attitude that makes a man an American.

The paramount role of the foreign-language paper is to help the member of whichever language community it serves to achieve this specific objective, to lose his identity as a foreigner and to become this American.

Americanism is something that belongs to the mind; it is not weight, color, height, race, religion or language except so far as each or any of these hinder or facilitate the attainment of this community of outlook that is meant when someone proudly proclaims: "I am an American." If it were merely a matter of documentation, of legalism, of possessing certain "papers" or documents, it wouldn't be worth fighting or dying for.

Exactly as affection and pride in the traditions and history of England are justifiable in any American

citizen of English ancestry, so is it for Americans of
other derivations, be they French or Spanish, Chinese
or Persian. But, in each case, the United States must
be the repository of the principal pride, the fundamental loyalty. The same is true for each of these foreign
languages.

The English language—perhaps it should be called
the American language—for it has developed so many
characteristics of its own, is historically and function-
ally our national language. There is no reason on
earth why any other language in which one has pride
and facility should not be this person's second language. Indeed, in our Twentieth Century world, every
American should learn more than his own language,
and how better to begin than to absorb, as fluently as
possible, the language of one's forefathers? But none
of these can also be our national language in the practical circumstances of our national existence, without
it critically injuring the subtle and delicate Americanization process.

Some theoreticians are inclined to shy away from
the expression "melting pot" as "old hat" and argue
that it is humiliating and even discriminatory. This is
to make mush of these words. The debate over this
was hotly argued, and honestly debated—in the open—
in some of our foreign-language press a generation or
so ago, and a decision reached. Far from belittling, it
was enlarging. Too bad that we haven't paid more
attention to our foreign-language newspapers!

No, the United States has been and is a great
"melting pot," and it is this which distinguishes it
from any other nation that ever existed on the face
of the earth, and for which each inhabitant of these

United States, and the world at large, has most to be thankful for on earth.

There are those who say that pride of country is "illiberal," too. They are the true illiberals, and the real conformists of our time, responsible for the confusion which would soften us up for history's coup de grace. Communism under such circumstances would only be the medium; we would, in hard, American lingo, "be asking for it."

The foreign-language press fits beautifully and heroically into this picture. Language, with all its handicaps in conveying exact ideas and precise motives, is nonetheless the medium most near perfection for communication between human beings. As such, for those persons whose understanding of English is still lacking or insufficient to communicate fully with the broad mass of people who make up this United States, the foreign-language press must serve as the channel and the liaison. This is its essential function.

The record shows that in spite of exceptions, even of treasonable exceptions such as the present communist press, our foreign-language newspapers have fulfilled this function well. In the process, all of us have undergone modification. So long as we abstain from making a hard mold, and saying this is the American for all time and under all circumstances, and insist on pouring the human clay into it, Americanization can proceed as a living process, producing the vital American type.

Our earliest history has proven that we fared best when we allowed flexibility and sufficient free-wheeling to take advantage of opportunities as they arise. This is the bold, American way. Nothing is more contrary, and un-American in character, than the committee system and what is called the planning approach, that would make soothsayers of us all, and bind us in conformist robes. Nothing is more contrary to team work and analysis as a basis for action.

This is the "melting pot." Those who tend its fires have grave responsibility, for it is a tremendous task, and requires the help of each American.

This, too, is the function of the foreign-language press, for the democratic idea is that which it is duty-bound to defend against the communist virus, or any other extremism. They all turn out alike, be they called nazism, fascism or communism. They all make the soul a prisoner.

Indeed, this is the responsibility the foreign-language editor has the least right to shirk. He and his people, whether they come from Europe or Asia, have been close to communism when not engulfed by it, and they know its contours and its sound, no matter what disguise they assume. They cannot escape the responsibility that goes with knowledge.